BLAZERS, BADGES AND BOATERS

BLAZERS, BADGES AND BOATERS

A PICTORIAL HISTORY OF SCHOOL UNIFORM

ALEXANDER DAVIDSON

SCOPE BOOKS

First published in Great Britain in 1990 by:
Scope Books Ltd
62 Murray Road
Horndean
Hants PO8 9JL

Phototypeset by Barbara James, Rowlands Castle, Hants
Printed by Richard Clay, Bungay, Suffolk

British Cataloguing in Publication Data

Blazers, badges and boaters : a pictorial history of school uniform.
1. Great Britain. Schools. Students. Uniforms, history
I. Davidson, Alexander, 1959-
687'.15

ISBN 0-906619-25-4

Acknowledgements

A book of this kind which seems to involve limitless research, can only be written with a great deal of help from others, in terms both of sharing memoirs and archives, and, more importantly, of emotional support.

First and foremost, I would like to record here my deep gratitude to my publisher Nicholas Pine for so untiringly helping me bring some order to the great mass of material, and turn it into a readable book.

I thank my parents for their great help in this project. Also Elizabeth Emanuel, the schoolgirl I met on the train, who pushed me into becoming a schoolteacher in the first place, and has explored with me untiringly over the years the sociological themes that form the basis for this book.

My extreme gratitude is due to Brian Nolan, head of Art at King's School Rochester, for the many long hours he has spent with me, passing on his valuable knowledge. My thanks too to Stanley Gregory, Headmaster of Chatham Grammar School for Boys, for encouraging the project.

In addition I am extremely grateful to Dr John Rae, ex-Head Master of Westminster School, for his enthusiastic interest in the book, and for the preface.

I thank Madeleine Harland for overseeing the complex editorial work with such diligence, and Geoffrey Stavert for reading the text with his usual scholarly attention to detail.

I acknowledge the great assistance of Mr M.K. Benson, archivist of Lewis's of Liverpool, in the provision of material and information which have helped this book see light of day. My extreme gratitude too to David Falcon of School Dinners, the unique London restaurant, for his provision of photographs and help generally. Likewise my great thanks are due to Ian Thomas of Eric Thomas Ltd for his unflagging support. I also thank House of Fraser for their help, and Mrs Lorna Poole, the archivist of the John Lewis Partnership for her constant interest in the project, and her willing provision of photographs.

I would like to acknowledge here too the help throughout the duration of this project of my dear friends Countess Dent, Paul Chynoweth, and Sebastian Payne.

My thanks to Paul Capra of Caps for his enthusiastic guided tour round his marvellous collection of caps.

May I take this chance to offer my heartfelt thanks to teachers and others associated with schools and relevant research bodies who have been unstinting in their help with the research for this project, in provision of photographs, and in the opening up of archives. Due to limited space, it has not been possible to mention everybody here, but the following in no particular order, have been particularly supportive and helpful:

Phyllis M. Sadler, Archivist, Ackworth School, Yorks; The Headmistress, Ancaster House School, Sussex.

Dr. M.D. Jones, The College, Bath Road, Cheltenham; David Sykes, Librarian, Bedales School, Petersfield; R.G. Miller, Archivist, Bedford School, Bedford; W.M. Sillery, Headteacher, Belfast Royal Academy; G.C. Smith, The Master, Belmont, The Mill Hill Junior School; Stephen G. Benson, Headmaster, Bishop's Stortford College; A.W. Wright, Headteacher, Bolton School (Boys Div); John Blackie, Muniments Room, Bradfield College; Eleanor Wooller, Archivist, The Girls' Grammar School, Bradford; Captain G.M. Tullis, Britannia Royal Naval College, Dartmouth; Mr. Evan Davies, Archivist, Britannia Royal Naval College, Dartmouth; Jeremy Bourne, Headmaster, Old School House, Bromsgrove School, Worcs.

Cadet Publications, Hull; Sister Julia Butcher, Headmistress, Cavendish School, Reading; Mrs. Isabel Raphael, Headmistress, The Channing School, London; Miss Doris Pritchard, Channing School, London; P.J. Attenborough, Headmaster, Charterhouse, Godalming; S. Gregory, Headmaster, Chetham Grammar School for Boys; Michael Powell, Librarian, Chetham's School of Music, Manchester; Paul Andrews, Second Master, Chetham's School of Music, Manchester; N.M. Plumley, Archivist, Christ's Hospital, Sussex; Neil Fleming, Master, Christ's Hospital School, Horsham; Mrs. J.D. Walters, Headmistress, Clifton High School for Girls, Bristol; Mr. Weir, Second Master, Colfe's School, London; Peter M. Heinecke, Archivist, Colfe's School, London.

C.R. Evans, Headteacher, Dauntsey's School, W. Lavington; Father Oliver Holt, The Walmesley Housemaster, Douai School; C.J. Linford, Headmaster, Downside School, Surrey; Mrs. R.M. Slythe, Head of Library, Dulwich College, London; M.A. Lang, Headteacher, Durham School.

C.J. Saunders, Headmaster, Eastbourne College; H.B. Harral, Eastbourne College; C.D. Waller, Headmaster, Eltham College, London; J.A. Read, Membership Treasurer, Old Elthamian's Association; P.F. Thomson, Headmaster, Emanuel School, London; Alan G. Scadding, Head of History, Epsom School, Surrey; W.E.K. Anderton, Head Master, Eton College, Windsor.

Sister Sylvia Cousins, Headteacher, Farnborough Hill Convent School, Hants; David R. Everett, Felsted School, Essex; T.M. Andrews, Headmaster, Felsted Preparatory School, Essex; James D. Cripps, Archivist, Forest School, Snaresbrook; Miss M.C. Atkins, Headmistress, Fort Pitt Grammar School for Girls, Kent; John C. Woods, Headmaster, The Friends' School, Saffron Walden.

K.P. Pearson, Principal, George Heriot's School, Edinburgh; Frank E. Gerstenberg, Principal, George Watson's College, Edinburgh; Nigel Mussett, Contingent Commander, CCF, Giggleswick School, Settle; Robert Waddell, Archivist, Gordonstoun School, Moray.

Mrs. I. Thomas, Assistant Librarian, Haileybury College, Hertford; Mrs. J.C. Lawrence, Headmistress, Harrogate College, Harrogate;

A.D.K. Hawkyard, Archivist, Harrow School; H.R. Walduck, The Harrow Association; Theodore Mallison, Archivist, Highgate School, London; Lt. Colonel H.S. Townend, Headmaster, Hill House, London; D.G. Ives, Headmaster, Holmewood House, Kent; John E. Liddell, Hutchesons' Former Pupils' Club Ltd.

Captain R.T. Youngman, captain Headmaster, Indefatigable, Gwynedd; Dr. John Blatchley, Headmaster, Ipswich School, Suffolk; David J. Woodhead, National Director, ISIS.

Mrs. B.H. Knighton, archivist, James Allen's Girls' School, London; Jo Wagerman, Headteacher, JFS Comprehensive School, London; Mr. D. Thomas, Managing Director, Jones & Park Ltd, Lancs.

John H. Duff, Rector, Kelvinside Academy, Glasgow; Elizabeth Foord, Keffolds Farm; R.J. Wicks, Headteacher, Kent College; Francis P. Moran, Headmaster, The King Alfred School, London; Mrs Molly Maxwell, old girl of The King Alfred School, London; Dr. R.W. Wilkinson, Headmaster, King Edward's School, Surrey; C. Dobson, Headmaster, King Edward VI School, Southampton; R.J. Henderson, head of history, King's College School, Cambridge; R.M. Reeve, Headmaster, King's College School, Wimbledon; Frank Miles, Archivist, King's College School, Wimbledon; Gordon W. Evans, Second Master, Kingston Grammar School, Surrey; A.H. Beadles, Headmaster, King's School, Burton; Paul Pollak, Second Master, The King's School, Canterbury; C.R.I. Matheson, Second Master, The King's School, Ely; Dr. John Moore, Headmaster, The King's School, Worcester.

Miss D.M.M. Stewart, Headmistress, Lawnside School, Great Malvern; F.A.D. Bland, Headmaster, The Licensed Victuallers' School, Slough; Andrew Wilson, teacher, The Licensed Victuallers' School, Slough; the Headteacher, London Nautical School; Adrian Luke, David Luke Ltd.

David R.C. West, Hon. Archivist, Marlborough College; Mrs. Christine Knight, Public Relations and Development Officer, Marymount School, Surrey; D.J. Skipper, Merchant Taylors' School, Middlesex; D.M. Sparforth, Headteacher, Merchiston Castle School, Edinburgh; John Hayward, Archivist, Monkton Combe Junior School, Bath; D. June Ellis, Headmistress, The Mount School York; Reverend J.F. Grumitt, Mount St. Mary's College, Sheffield.

Mr. J. Dolman, Chief Executive, The National Children's Wear Association; Mrs. J.L. Clanchy, Headmistress, North London Collegiate School for Girls.

C.R.F. Potter, Headmaster, Old Swinford Hospital, Stourbridge; Don W. Walsh, Secretary, Old Williamson Club; T. McIntyre, The Oratory School, Reading.

M.R.H. Scott, estates manager, Portora Royal School, Co. Fermanagh.

Dr. R. Gliddon, Headteacher, Queen Elizabeth's Hospital, Bristol.

Anthony B.E. Hudson, Acting Warden, Radley College, Oxon; Miss E. Castle, Headmistress, The Red Maids' School, Bristol; David J. Jewell, Headmaster, Repton School, Derby; Mrs. Marian Green, Deputy Headmistress, The Grammar School for Girls, Rochester; Mrs Harriet Topping, Archivist, Roedean School, Brighton; Peter W. Bennett, Vicemaster, Rossall School, Lancs; A.A. Horne, Royal Hospital School,

Ipswich; Naomi Tarrant, Curator of Costume and Textiles, Royal Museum of Scotland; Diana Otter, Headmistress, The Royal Naval School, Haslemere; R.D. Balaam, Headteacher, Royal Russell School, Croydon; Mrs. P.J. Macrory, Librarian, Rugby School, Warwickshire; P.F. Watkinson, Headteacher, Rydal School, Colwyn Bay.

C. Bernard Waldron OSB, Headmaster, St. Augustine's College, Westgate-on-Sea; Father Lawrence, St. Benedict's School, Ealing; A.J. Pull, Headmaster, St. Edmund's School, Hindhead; J.C. Phillips, The Warden, St. Edward's School, Oxon; J.W. Tate, Archivist, St. Edward's School, Oxon; A.H. Mould, Headteacher, St. John's College School, Cambridge; J.H. Binfield, Headmaster, St. Lawrence's College in Thanet, Ramsgate; Mrs. L.E. James, Headmistress, St. Leonard's School, Fife; Sister Jean Sinclair, Headmistress, St. Leonards-Mayfield School, East Sussex; Mrs. J.P.G. Smith, Headmistress, St. Mary's School, Gerrard's Cross; M.D. Martin, Bursar, and Brian Jones, Archivist, St. Mary's School, Brighton; Mrs. Eleanor Denton, former Archivist, St. Paul's Boy's School, London; D.A. Sutton, Headmaster, St. Paul's Cathedral Choir School; Mrs. Heather Brigstocke, High Mistress, St. Paul's Girls' School, London; Andrew P. Blumer, Headmaster, St. Piran's School, Berks; F.E. Maidment, Headmaster, Shrewsbury School; John Warmington, librarian, Sherborne School, Dorset; Thomas Leimdorfer, Sidcot School, Avon; Geoffrey Fowler, Archivist, Silcoates School; John Winstanley, deputy Headmaster, Sir Thomas Rich's, Gloucester; A.C. Baldwin, Headmaster, Slindon College, Sussex; James G. Marshall, Archivist, Stamford School, Essex; Edward Gaven, Sutton Valence School, Kent.

B.B. Sutton, Headmaster, Taunton School, Somerset; C.H.D. Everett, Headmaster, Tonbridge School, Kent; Mr. H. Barry Orchard, Tonbridge School Kent.

G.D. Slaughter, Headmaster, University College School, London; Bryan Matthews, secretary, Uppingham Association, Uppingham School, Rutland; N.R. Bomford, Headmaster, Uppingham School, Rutland.

Avril Hart, Textiles Department, Victoria and Albert Museum, London. Miss D. Swatman, Headmistress, Wadhurst College, Sussex; Alan Grigg, Headmaster, Wellington School, Ayr; Mrs. Alison Fincham, Archivist, Wellington College, Crowthorne; Dr. D.H. Newsome, Headmaster, Wellington College, Crowthorne; J MacG. K. Kendall-Carpenter, Headteacher, Wellington School, Somerset; Mrs. Jocelyn Henfrey, Librarian, Wells Cathedral School, Somerset; L.G. Roland-Adams, Headmaster, Westminster Abbey Choir School, London; John Field, Librarian, Westminster School, London; Frederick Percy, Hon Archivist, Whitgift School, Croydon; P.D. Briggs, Headteacher, William Hulme's Grammar School; J.P. Sabben-Clare, Headmaster, Winchester College, Winchester; A. de M. Beanland, Worksop College, Notts; J.H. Ancell, Headmaster, Wrekin College, Telford; Betty Jackson, house-mistress, Wycliffe College.

Foreword

by
JOHN RAE

There is one chapter missing from this richly detailed and entertaining book. It is a chapter on school uniform as the headteacher's nightmare. As I recall, there was no other topic more likely to be regarded as a touchstone of discipline. The state of the pupils' dress was thought to reflect the state of the school. Academic results might be excellent, sporting achievements better than ever, but if the boys wore their shirt-tails outside their trousers and their ties like nooses loosely slung about their necks, then something was fundamentally wrong. By the same token, parents have not infrequently been taken in by outward ap-pearances, mistaking a smartly turned out student body for an efficient and happy school.

There *is* a connection between the way a school looks and the quality of education it offers. Litter, graffiti, vandalism, scruffily attired staff as well as pupils all suggest a lack of good leadership and of pride in the community. A head who turns a blind eye is not being liberal; he is being lazy. The problem is faces is how to achieve a reasonable standard of tidiness without concentrating all his authority on what is after all a superficial aspect of school life.

Superficial or not, school uniform is part of the history of British schools. Its origins lie not in the great public schools for the children of the rich but in the charity schools for the children of the poor. The monastic cassock worn by the pupils of Christ's Hospital in the 16th century was probably the first school uniform. It was not until the 19th century that the fee-paying public schools adopted the idea.

The reason for their conversion was simple. The old public schools had been anarchic places in which the young aristocrats dressed as they wished and played their – voluntary – games in whatever worn and battered gear was to hand. Uniformity of dress was one of the consequences of the movement to replace anarchy with order. Along with compulsory games, stricter supervision of the pupils' lives and morals, and a broadening of the classical curriculum, school uniform was an essential characteristic of the reformed public schools.

Once the idea took hold, it soon became an obsession. The many new public schools founded in Victorian England used a distinctive uniform as a way of establishing their social status. Wherever the public school tradition spread overseas, school uniform was de rigueur. As the number of state schools grew after the 1870 Education Act, the grammar schools put their pupils into uniform to distinguish them from the pupils at the less sought after elementary and secondary modern schools. Even today, comprehensive schools that wish to be associated with the grammar school tradition prescribe a blazer in the school colours. Having started as a badge of poverty, school uniform became a mark of social ambition.

It was in the boys public schools, however, that uniform was used to delineate status within the school itself. In a peculiarly English fashion, uniform defined the hierarchy and reminded the new boy of the deference he owed to the prefect and the 'blood'. When I started teaching at a public school in 1955, the unwritten rules about dress – how many buttons done up on the blazer, what angle to wear the straw hat – were still used to underpin the ladder of rank and privilege.

The Sixties put an end to all that. There had been schoolboy rebellions against uniform in the past and the Second World War had killed off some of the more expensive or ludicrous items, but it was the widespread youth revolt of the late Sixties that had the greatest impact. In most schools, uniform remained, though modified in the direction of informality. The sillier hierarchical touches disappeared. A few public schools abolished uniform altogether and later regretted it. The two most distinctive uniforms – those of Eton and Christ's Hospital – were largely unchanged, perhaps because they were so eccentric it was difficult to know what on earth to change to.

School uniform remains a source of 'niggle' between the pupils and the school authorities. It would be odd indeed if this were not the case. But it is wrong to imagine that the adolescent rebel really wants uniform to be abolished or that abolition would put a stop to the arguments. I taught for a term in a private school in New York where uniform had been replaced by a dress code agreed by the authorities and the pupils. Far from reducing disputes about what could or could not be worn, the dress code was open to more conflicting interpretations than the uniform regulations had ever been.

The debate about school uniform is full of such paradoxes. I suspect the British will always be ambivalent, not sure whether uniform encourages positive attitudes or dull conformity, humility or arrogance, equality or social pretension. Which is why it remains such an intriguing subject. No one would claim that school uniform is a matter of profound social or historical importance, but it tells us something about our national attitudes as well as about our education system. It deserves a book – not too heavy, not too flip – and I am delighted that Alexander Davidson and Scope Books have provided one.

JOHN RAE
Former Head Master of Westminster School

*You send your child to the schoolmaster,
but 'tis the schoolboys who educate him.
You send him to the Latin class, but
much of his tuition comes, on his way to
school, from the shop-windows.*

Emerson: Conduct of Life, *Culture*

Contents

Chapter One

BRANDED FOR LIFE

Just as we're all what we eat, so schoolchildren are surely what they wear.

Nowadays, the whining schoolboy, with his satchel and shining morning face, may creep unwillingly to school right up to his sixteenth year, but at least he's more comfortably dressed than his Elizabethan predecessor.

Sixteenth century schoolchildren served as guinea-pigs for the earliest experiments in uniform; charity pupils wearing bulky cassock-like cloaks with fussy trimmings from the Christ's Hospital model. The scholars looked like little monks, and before breeches were added in 1786, they must have suffered, so one researcher put it, as Highland soldiers reputedly do.

This charity uniform, unwieldly as it was, lingers today. Chetham Hospital School for the musically gifted, to take one example, revived in the early seventies the chic Tudor costume it had started with in 1654. Not surprisingly, in the contemporary climate of fashion, the girls resented missing out on miniskirts.

But school uniform, naturally conservative as it may be, has been forced to keep some sort of pace with the ebb and flow of change. For the Reverend Wallace Clare, who cared for the old school uniforms enough to write a book singing their praises, trendy innovations in style appear nothing short of heresy.

His text, manifestly a labour of love, is steeped in such rhetoric as this:

> It is to be hoped that the governors of the schools in question may be inspired to re-introduce the old historic costumes, above all if these happened to be of the Tudor school.

Eton boys still wear elegant tailcoats with black waistcoats, striped trousers and snazzy bow or tape white ties. The present Head Master is correct in calling this getup the ordinary morning dress of the Victorian gentleman. With all the public attention this attire has provoked, it is hardly surprising that old Etonians are so confident a breed. The value of this dress ingredient in their educational diet has inspired countless imitators. Hence, for instance, the widespread appeal of the Eton suit.

To insist on uniform is of course to insist on standards of dress, but it is also evidence of an inability to consider those standards in terms other than those of uniform. A supplier once expressed the widely held view that we could not have our children going to school in jeans, like the Americans. Well, too bad – the corruption has already set in; inside some

A 20th century pupil from Colfe's School, London SE12 meeting his 17th century counterpart in an imaginative drawing by C.J. Folkard.

Pupils of Christ's Hospital putting their feet up in front of House.

Two charity boys of Chetham's Hospital, Manchester engrossed in a book.

ILEA schools for instance, as well as some top independent schools, such as St. Paul's Girls' School.

Such is the impact of uniform that adults nurture grudges when the bugbear has in practical terms long since ceased to encroach upon their lives. Antonia White, for instance, recalls Lippington's neurotic precautions which the nuns insisted the girls took before having a bath. Although the bathroom doors were locked, this famous author-to-be had to wrap her body in a calico cloak which tied round her neck and hung in heavy folds to her feet. While this turned washing into an obstacle course, it successfully prevented her from catching a glimpse of her body. The long-term effects are obvious in her autobiographical novels.

A child's pangs about uniform that is not quite right can be disproportionately severe. Arthur Marshall refers to a prep. school boy's horror that his grey flannel suit seems darker or lighter than those of his friends, or that his tuckbox is of different dimensions.

The same writer evokes the agony girls suffer when their mothers insist they must make do with what, in their eyes, isn't uniform at all. As he points out, one flat-chested girl even asked her mother for a 'bust-bodice', not to wear, but just to own, as other girls had them.

For pupils of the eighties at Highgate School, the main aim in life is to jump on to the latest fashion bandwagon and to wear white socks, an aberration which the more enlightened housemasters know better than to forbid.

The anti-uniform lobby carries the liberal process of thought still further, arguing that even the wearing of second-hand uniform may brand children with lifelong inferiority complexes.

Rituals such as the prep. school custom of removing shirt and vest after putting on pyjama-bottoms help to develop a modesty which may likewise develop into an adult obsession.

Any prostitute with an eye for big money certainly keeps school skirts, shorts and gymslips in her wardrobe for the benefit of her upper-class clientele – barristers, politicians, and other such public irreproachables. Cards advertising these specialist services are regularly displayed in London's West End newsagents at an inflated weekly rate and, with the same telephone numbers, in London 'phone boxes for free. The demand is there, and so perhaps it is as well somebody has cashed in on it.

A good many historians have made their living out of the gamut of sexual interests in which the Ancient Greeks indulged – the more openly the better, and certainly with more outlets than our own legislature has ever cared to sanction. Even Zeus was represented as a rapist, and poets such as Socrates favoured young whores of the same sex. Significantly, perhaps, the Hellenic schoolchild wore no uniform.

Generally, a uniform that is easy on the flesh must be more welcome than the itchy or overtight alternative, although fashion (or prejudice against it) has been all too often the criterion for selection. It is noticeable that adolescent boys will accept dress restrictions which would drive girls of the same age to distraction.

A pupil of Royal Hospital, Ipswich with a large cannon used at Trafalgar, c.1860.

This 1860 photograph of The Royal Hospital, Ipswich is one of the earliest of a schoolroom on record.

Gardening in gymslips for pupils of James Allen's girls school, Dulwich, 1900s.

The dining room at Forest School, Snaresbrook, London, 1939.

Increasingly schools have abolished, and more still have relaxed, their uniform requirements. Many public schools such as Ampleforth and Wellington now demand little uniform beyond smart casual wear, and neither academic nor social standards seem to suffer as a result.

In recent years, a few comparatively enterprising headteachers have encouraged pupils to unravel the uniform problem at its roots, and to design their own uniforms. One head justified such liberalism by his unfashionable wish that girls should not leave his school initiated only into the jolly hockey-sticks mentality. Certainly, in the field of business, an attractive personal appearance will pay more dividends than past scholastic or athletic prowess in one of the world's mere nurseries. It is a pity more headteachers do not see this. It took A.S. Neill, Summerhill School's rebel headmaster, to point out that the man who prides himself too much on uniform is usually a second-best fellow who values the second-best in life.

If we need uniform to control our pupils, there is surely something drastically wrong. In continental schools, which do not usually have uniforms, academic and disciplinary standards are often higher. Can this be entirely a coincidence?

Why then do we retain uniform, come hell or high water, a priority never so in evidence as in the thick of wartime deprivation? Uniform is not, after all, the only instrument for inculcating the herd instinct, although it is without a doubt one of the most powerful.

Boys of Monkton Combe Junior School, Bath, wearing their Eton suits one Sunday, 1934.

Dolls from the collection at Licensed Victuallers School, Slough representing the childrens dress of c.1837 (above) and c.1897 (right).

As one researcher puts it, public school boys are more easily controlled if you force them to be the same, and uniform furthers this by stamping individuals with the image of an institution. In this context, an Eton head said:

> What we in the public schools aim at producing is a type of man who can be trusted to pull his weight at any job that he is given, who has learnt not to consider his own interests as important as those of the institution he serves, who believes, rightly or wrongly, that there are some great and solid virtues which his country (or if you like his school) possesses, and is anxious that its reputation should not suffer in his keeping.

Small but significant distinctions in uniform broadcast rank within a school, shaping attitudes that have been known to linger in adult life. Just as scholars have been traditionally favoured with insignia or gowns, so team members parade their silks and colours. Prefects wear their distinctive ties loosely knotted. Sixth formers take natural advantage of relaxed dress regulations. These are sometimes so flexible as to enable them to dissociate themselves from the school. Spectacular arms, with Latin mottos, which even a schoolchild could construe if he wished, denote lineage that is sometimes recondite.

Social propriety has played its modest part in the evolution of uniform, although usually in retrospect an absurd one. When bicycles made their debut in the eighteen nineties, schoolgirls' skirts naturally had to be widened. For obvious reasons, the hems were weighted with lead.

Uniform may well represent an unseen, so insidious, mode of social control. Wober offers us a plausible enough theory that just as tribal societies use body paint to reduce personal identity during the transitory adolescent phase, so we exploit school uniform.

Granted that our dependence on school uniform is ritualistic, how have we coped with the restrictions, and how adeptly have we pioneered its historical phases? Under what circumstances have we most cherished this so British institution, and when have we been happier to disown it?

Given the sad dearth of literature on the subject, our national obsession with school uniform has been sublimated almost exclusively into fitting out our children immaculately and expensively for school. The historical tradition, like the working of our sewer system, has generally not been inquired into but taken for granted.

The scanty writings available on this subject so dear to our hearts seem too often to skirt round the subject, and are devastatingly dull to boot. The purpose of this book is to plug the gap in our social history.

Charles Lamb paid uncertain homage to the uniform ritual when he wrote 'His very garb as it is antique and venerable feeds his self respect.' We must probe the traditions just as he did, and draw our more modern conclusions.

Chapter 2

UNIFORM FOR THE POOR

The early charity school uniform was designed to emphasise the low status of the children who wore it. The original style as used at Christ's Hospital in the sixteenth century served as a prototype. Originally russet, it converted after only a year to blue, which was the colour characteristically worn by the servile classes. The uniform survives today, virtually unchanged, in Christ's Hospital, and in a number of other charity schools.

The cassock was the mainstay of the charity school dress. What was its pedigree? Holbein's sketches showing the epaulette at the shoulder refute religious origins, but the cassock certainly looked like a monastic habit, and the children who wore it were expected to conduct themselves with the iron discipline of the monks whom they resembled.

The charity children were also expected to stay clean, and it was quite in the spirit of their cloth that their petticoats were yellow to discourage vermin, 'by the reason the white cottons is said to breed the same'. The demise of the 'yellows' in 1865 was greeted with joy. As D.J. Walkins in his history of Sir Thomas Rich's School put it:

> This was a sensible move. The boys probably regarded them as nothing but a nuisance, as they must have been constricting when walking, since the gown itself, normally worn without the petticoat, opened to the waist to allow easy movement.

The yellow stockings worn by charity children were at one stage nicknamed 'mustard pots', while the cassock went through a phase of being called a 'tea cosy'. However, to compensate for its freakish appearance, the uniform had a traditional dignity, and a lot of warmth, which was why some schools retained it as uniform.

It is also true to say that the charity uniform has undergone slight modifications over the years to make it look more stylish. Brass buttons inscribed with Edward VI's head replaced hooks and eyes on the Christ's Hospital uniform in 1706, while breeches were provided there firstly for the 'sick and weakly' who had suffered 'great inconveniency' for their want, and later for all pupils.

Shoes at Christ's Hospital, originally laced, later became buckled, while the cap switched from bright red to an aggressive black, then was subsequently abolished altogether.

At one stage, Christ's Hospital pupils wore large tabs and pins with ordinary collars, and a matron of Christ's Hospital (1736) once stole 207,082 pins worth £10.7s. Today's pupils wear instead a 'strategically

A typical Christ's Hospital pupil in Victorian times.

A Blue Coat boy of the state subsidised Sir Thomas Rich's School, Gloucester, 1881. A silver medallion bearing his own number hangs from his chest.

Contemporary girls of Christ's Hospital school in their standard cassocks and coloured stockings.

A pupil of Christ's Hospital School, Horsham.

placed' button and tabs. Another feature of the Christ's Hospital uniform has been the girdle of red leather, stamped with the founder's head, and with the figure of a Christ's Hospital boy.

Pupils on whom it has been forced have often sneered at the charity uniform, whereas adults in contrast have often fallen in love with its appearance. Typical is this eulogy (1687) on the part of John Evelyn:

> There were nearly 800 boys and girls, so decently clad, cleanly lodged... that I was delighted to see the progress some little youths of thirteen or fourteen years have made.

The charity uniform had a particular purpose of identifying the class of children who wore it. As the rules for London Charity Schools said:

> When the children are cloathed they wear their caps, bands and cloaths every day; whereby the Trustees, Benefactors and others may know and see what their behaviour is abroad.

Sadly wearers were constantly reminded of what Bishop Butler referred to as their 'servile state', and this state was exploited. The pathos of the child dressed in charity uniform made demands on the public purse. Fund raising operations were successfully organised by groups such as the Society for Promoting Christian Knowledge, but perhaps the most lucrative technique was to place statues of charity children with collection boxes outside church doors.

Wearers of charity dress suffered from being paraded like cattle, in order to raise funds, through the streets of Bristol, or before audiences with vested interest as at the annual dinners of the Philanthropic Society.

In order to win over the public's heart, the charity dress had to look attractive, and this was sometimes taken to absurd lengths, as in the case highlighted in the article 'London Charities' in *The Illustrated London News* (1842) where the Charterhouse boy's gown was criticised for its long hanging sleeve 'never intended for use but which adds considerably to the picturesque appearance of the wearer'.

If picturesque, charity dress is also demeaning. Dr. Isaac Watts declared that charity schools ought to teach children their place in life, and their clothes are an obvious medium for this. As John Locke explained in his 'thoughts covering education' (1693):

> [If children wore shoes] which like those of the poor let in water, they would never take cold, for the poor who are so used to wet feet take no more cold or harm by it than if they were wet by their hands.

Particularly degrading was the system prevalent in the Victorian era of identifying charity children by numbers. *The Workman's Guide* argued that this was 'a great saving of memory, time, and trouble'. In Charles Dickens' classic novel *Dombey and Son*, the infamous Mr. Dombey talks of a charity child's number 'as if he were a hackney coach', and shows how charity children were treated as objects. Old habits die hard – boys of Christ's Hospital up to 1721 wore brass tickets tied to their coats if they left the school premises, and this tradition lingered into our century, when masters have given imaginary tickets to boys wanting leave.

Charity children were given special punishments that affected their dress. Miscreants at Ratcliffe School were made to wear everyday dress on Sundays. The fool's coat at Greenwich School, and the yellow punishment coat at St Martin-in-the-Field's School (1771) were dreaded punishments for recalcitrant charity children.

Uniquely, idlers at York Spinning School had wool pinned to their shoulders, or gowns turned inside out, and were threatened that: 'If she be not more careful, she shall be exhibited to her patroness.' More flamboyantly, pupils who left the premises of Grey Coat Girls' School without matron's leave of absence, were forced to wear a jacket with a red R on it, and on a second offence were actually handcuffed.

Charity children were sometimes permitted to atone for their naughtiness by methods kinder on the cloth – such as begging a fool's pardon in public, or standing in the middle of the classroom to be mocked at.

Although most charity children suffered in silence, there was one who poured out his sartorial sorrows to Punch (1868).

> Please Sir, Mr. Punch, will you have a shy at our old Governors, and make them change our togs and dress like other fellows, and not go about like girls in those old stupid stuffy gowns, which stick so to our legs that we have to tuck 'em up whenever we play football... And then in summertime you know our gowns are beastly hot and heavy, and cling about one so that of course one can't play cricket.

A few defended the charity uniforms on prestige grounds which may have been spurious. In an article on Christ's Hospital, Charles Lamb commends the charity boy's aloofness:

A group of Chetham's Hospital boys wearing their distinctive hats.

A pupil in the less glamorous charity costume of Old Swinford Hospital, 1916.

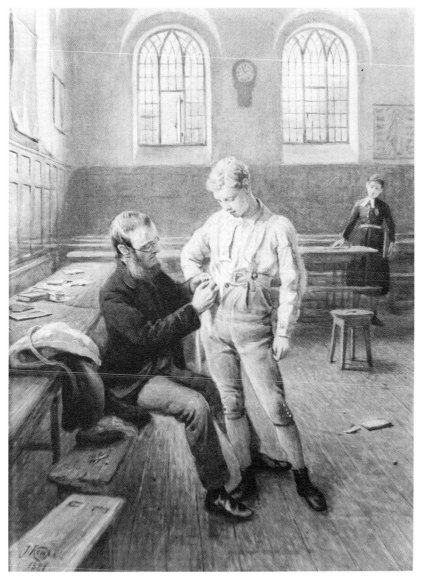

A charity pupil of Sir Thomas Rich's School, Gloucester being carefully measured up by a tailor as depicted in this 1882 watercolour by J. Kemp.

> Lest by overhastily mixing with the common and secular playfellows, he should commit the dignity of his cloth.

Just as charity children were constrained by their cloth, so were their parents. The St. Leonard's School, Shoreditch went so far as to insist that children whose clothes were stolen by their parents would be ignominiously expelled from school, on grounds that charity clothes were school property.

Charity uniform not only belonged to the school, but was often manufactured on the premises by schoolgirls who were put to work sewing it in needlework classes. In contrast, charity clothes provided from outside were often of a poor standard, due to the attitude of tradesmen who refused to treat charity children like human beings. This was why, for instance, the shoes and breeches supplied to Blue Coat boys at Sir Thomas Rich's School in the early 19th century were of such a poor quality.

Of course, some charity children were more dubious than others, and doubtless helped cast a shadow on the species. In one particularly nasty case at Sir Thomas Rich's School, one Master John Brown stabbed a fellow pupil with a knife. Here is a revealing extract from his confidential medical report:

> They had a long conversation with the boy himself and made enquiry of the master respecting him. They are of the opinion that although the boy is in many respects mentally deficient, there is no sufficient reason why he should be dismissed from school.

Charity children remain fundamentally charity children even after they have grown up and spread their wings. The Foundling Hospital, for instance, issued boys who left with a parchment inscribed as follows:

> You were... quite helpless, forsaken, poor, and deserted. But of charity you have been fed, clothed and instructed.

It was intended that they should remember this for life.

Chapter 3

ONE UPMANSHIP IN UNIFORM

Children in a given school will all wear essentially the same uniform, but there will be minor variations. These are particularly prominent in the colours and styles of caps and ties for instance, awarded sometimes for achievement in school sports.

Likewise academic prowess is acknowledged by privileges in dress. Just as George IV claimed he could recognise people who were not gentlemen by the way that they divided their coats when they sat down, so the rugby-playing hearty has always been able to spot the scholar by his black gown, the oldest existing version of which survives at Winchester, unchanged since 1394.

Scholars may wear distinctive badges, which at St. Paul's Boys' School take the form of a beautiful silver pike. This fish, now hallmarking the scholar's badge, was engraved on the watch chain in the Victorian era. The fish was a vital early Christian symbol, in Ancient Greece *ichthus*, an acronym for: 'Jesus Christ son of God, Saviour'. It was obviously felt that there was something saintly in being a scholar. The classical tradition was also important at St. Paul's. As Dr. Sleuth, High Master in the 1840s, put it:

> At St. Paul's we teach nothing but the classics: nothing but Latin and Greek. If you want your boy to learn anything else, you must have him taught at home, and for this purpose we give him three half-days a week.

Latin and Greek were still more familiar to the Christians in Ancient Rome, who carved this precious fish on their tombstones. Just as there were 153 fishes in the Biblical miraculous draught, so 153 scholars were originally permitted at St. Paul's. Whether this was coincidence or design, it has certainly endowed the silver fish with a sacred flavour.

Indeed, St. Paul's scholars with their silver pikes cut an impressive figure. As an old boy of the Edwardian era put it:

> I felt envious of those clever boys who had won scholarships to the school, and so were entitled to a silver fish.

Instead of a silver fish, a silver pen was awarded to scholars of Colfe's Grammar School, but this did not have the same religious overtones. Colfe's scholars would wear these pens in their hats for only six-week stretches at a time, whereas St. Paul's boys would bear their silver fish badges all the year round.

Nonetheless, to give it due credit, Colfe's silver pen was not easily won. Every year, eight Colfe's scholars had to engage in difficult debates, entirely in Latin, before a learned selection panel, and the three

An elite body of Marlborough College, 1862.

Members of Pop at Eton College, 1933, standing on the steps up to their classroom. Pop is a self-electing school disciplinary/elite body, founded as a debating society in 1811.

top debaters would be offered the prize pen. Doubtless the winners would put their fluency at Latin to good everyday use, since Latin was the only language officially spoken during the school day.

It is doubtless resentment of privileges afforded to scholars that has led to their frequent ostracism from the rest. Scholars at Marlborough College in the 1920s for instance were kept at arm's length, and labelled 'aesthetes' and 'swots'.

Eton scholars perhaps suffered the most, in a system hardly designed to pamper the frail and studious. They had to keep an eye out for bullies every day, and be prepared to fight or run. In particular, their top hats were constantly kicked about, and they didn't have the means to repair the damage.

Scholars will sometimes react violently to persecution. These days, many scholars of The King's School, Canterbury discard their gowns after a short period of wearing them. Who nowadays wants to be branded with the mark of the scholar?

Far more exciting a proposition is to wear the special uniform of prefects as this signifies power and freedom. As a master at Eastbourne College (1900s) explained:

> My nephew once invited me to visit him at school,
> To see the inner working of a newly published rule,
> 'Twas graven on the mantelpiece, 'twas written on the shelves,
> "Take care of Prefects and the rest must take care of themselves..."

Eton fags serving senior boys at table in this 1850 lithograph by George Robert Winter, Our Mess of My Dames.

> There were so many things a Prefect had to do,
> They had to ask the Head for halves, design a cap or two,
> To edit the School Magazine, or take an hour's Prep.
> That they really must be excused their 'books' and 'prose' and 'prep'.

There is some feeling within schools that prefects cannot be expected to exercise their full functions without being dressed for the part. As one old boy of St. Paul's said:

> Manners makyth man is a very sound maxim, but I am not sure that the clothes have not something to do with the making.

On the downside, however, the prefect's clothes can give him an exaggerated sense of his own importance. As W.H. Auden, an ex-schoolmaster himself, put it:

> A really good prefect is as rare as a comet. Authority makes most boys of eighteen or any other age into stuck up little idiots.

The prefect's most terrifying insignia of authority, albeit on the periphery of school uniform, is the cane. Its swishing sound is enough to set many a junior's teeth on edge, even if it is not applied to his back seat.

The cane, when it is applied, proves a far harsher instrument of punishment in the hands of an eighteen year old boy than in those of a doddering old schoolmaster. However, sadism and sexual thrills have been known to motivate both. If canes were not available, walking sticks would do, and prefects at Haileybury College were wont to put the latter to full use.

The cane that is strictly symbolic has its place, particularly in the Cathedral schools. The head boy of King's School, Rochester is the proud bearer of a lordly malacca cane on whose silver bands names of past school heads are inscribed. The vice head and heads of house there bear canes too. Schools such as The King's School, Canterbury and Harrow sustain similar traditions.

Besides the cane, a curious motley collection of distinctions in and insignia of dress are available to prefects. At Rochester Grammar School, they have worn silver badges; at St. Edmund's, Canterbury, white jumpers, and at St. Joseph's Convent, Abbey Wood, gold-striped ties. At Whitgift School, prefects had their own caps and ties.

There are countless variations on these themes, but two particularly interesting cases are those of the prefects at Chatham Grammar School who wore special striped hatbands, in imitation of the Winchester system, and the Radley College prefects who were permitted to wear their gowns over the shoulders.

As trivial, or even absurd as these little sartorial honours might appear in the adult perspective, they are made to matter greatly to children. It is the kind of confidence trick inflicted upon children which has become part of our culture. A former pupil of Oxford Central Girls' School here enthusiastically recalls:

> Most of us were prefects or held other offices. We sported rather distinguished looking ties and prowled like gods among the rest.

Dress privilege, although providing powerful support to prefects, is not in itself all they need. Prefects who rely on looking the part may come a

The school head of Winchester College wearing a scholar's gown; the coloured velvet edging is a mark of his office.

cropper as the Master of Wellington College was to discover. One historian put it like this:

> Benson might clothe his Classical XI in top hats and give them a stick to carry, but he could not endow them with extra years, and it was not easy for a young boy who had risen to the top very quickly to control boys older and physically more powerful than himself.

Children in the top forms at school, even if not prefects, have been awarded privileges in what they wear. For instance, sixth formers at Uppingham and Sir Joseph Williamson's Mathematical School have been allowed to wear boaters. These were in fact resented, partly because they had been originally worn in orphanages.

More popular were the tailcoats and top hats worn by eighth formers (the equivalent to sixth formers) at St. Paul's Boys' School.

One of the most absurd criteria for wearing uniform was the pupil's height. For instance, at St. Paul's School, boys were only allowed to wear boaters when they were personally at least six feet tall, and they had to be measured against a wall to check this. More just were the regulations at Harrow and Eton in the 1930s, where boys had to be over five foot six and five foot four in height to discard their Eton suits. During this period, girls at Roedean School could wear stockings only after they were five foot tall. Possibly pupils in certain schools of this era who were, through no fault of their own, short in stature, grew up with inferiority complexes.

Children of the pre-Second World War years were drawn like magnets to the many sham formulae for increasing height that were advertised for sale at the time. The absurdity of school uniform regulations encouraged the con man to prey on children desperate to grow taller, and on their sometimes no less gullible parents.

Sixth formers at Christ's Hospital School for Girls (c. 1910) wore black aprons and were called black apes. Sixth formers at Marlborough College (1920s) could put hands in pockets at will; a privilege indeed. At Bermondsey School, prefects wore their own choice of clothes, and at Christ's Hospital a broad girdle.

Many dress regulations are futile upholders of school tradition. Take for instance these regulations from the rulebook of Harrow (1930s):

> New men have no privileges. Second years wear all their coat buttons but one undone, and may turn their collars up.
> Third years may undo all their coat buttons, and may wear stiff turndown collars, silk scarves, and coloured socks.
> Fourth years may wear grey flannel waistcoats, silk ends to their tails, brown shoes, and buttonholes.
> Bloods may wear fancy waistcoats and patent leather shoes.

Pupils had to obey such ridiculous rules, and resented it. The glamour was obvious only to onlookers. As a boy, the actor Cardew Robinson went to Harrow County Secondary School, from whose grounds he was able to watch the house matches of Harrow School adjacent. He describes here his feelings at the time:

> I used to sit with legs dangling, absorbed in their matches, my emotions a mixture of admiration and envy.

A boy lighting his fag master's fire at Eton College, 1940.

He envied those sons of gentry no less than his teachers did.

The worst indignities of dress are reserved for pupils at the lower end of the school. Traditionally fags have always been stigmatised by their dress, which at Winchester College took the form of waistcoats especially manufactured to carry writing instruments for their elders and betters. Fags of Charterhouse fared worse, having their jackets ripped up during 'football in cloisters', an invented game they were forced to play, while fags of Eton College wiped dishes with their surplices and carried coals in their gowns.

Endowed with the most impressive uniform privileges and most prestigious insignia of all pupils were those belonging to a self elected elite within the school. Eton's Pop is probably the best known, and its members have traditionally worn spongebag trousers, brightly patterned waistcoats, and hats ornamented with sealing wax. Members have sometimes competed to look different, and one would secretly unravel his waistcoat cloth every day in order to create ever varying patterns. What a poseur he was!

No less flamboyant are the butterfly bow ties and shiny coat buttons, fastened with link pins, that have been worn by members of Harrow's prestigous Philathletic Committee. These members and other Harrovians even nowadays wear gaudy waistcoats at prizegivings.

Less flamboyant but certainly as distinctive are the coats of superior blue jersey, the soft breeches, and the velvet cuffs, together with a full fourteen large silver buttons worn by the Grecians, a similar elite body at Christ's Hospital.

Some schools retain special uniform distinctions amongst all pupils, and not just for seniors. King's School, Rochester probably has a more diverse and more colourful uniform than any other school in England. Only recently was its custom of removing straw hats while passing between classrooms abandoned, but other extraordinary and picturesque customs appertaining to school uniform are retained. For instance, members of the King's School Debating Society, known as Zetountes, wear striking green needlecord waistcoats with brass buttons. Members of the art and music societies there likewise wear specific uniforms. In school life, all this has great significance, although it must be borne in mind that real artists and musicians are less concerned with such distinctive trappings.

The variety of ties worn at King's School, Rochester is particularly great. King's scholars wear silver ties with a red Tudor rose, music scholars maroon ties with a silver rose, and minor scholars black ties with a rose. Choristers wear green, black and red ties, while the old boys are entitled to wear black, blue and white ties with a red line, or with a purple line if they had boarded at the school.

What is our healthiest reaction to all these sartorial distinctions? Surely we cannot rebuke the seventeen year old Compton Mackenzie for coming to this conclusion:

> If you think I'm going to hang on at school, just for the pleasure of wearing a round cap with a white button on top, or even a cap with a tassel, you'd better think again.

We must question, as he did, whether dress privilege really matters. It was Pindar who defined the wise as knowing things by nature (phua) and the foolish as those depending on a formal education (mathontes). Never have his words made so much sense, in the sartorial context, as now.

Chapter 4

UNIFORM FOR THE HEAD

School hats worn various ways, and put to uses manufacturers have not dreamed of, have enabled wearers to poke fun at the uniform regulations, Earlier this century, new boys at Shrewsbury School, for instance, would pull their Homburg hats over their noses, which made them look like so many Paddington bears, the raffish element wearing brown hats instead of grey.

Rebellious ways of wearing school headgear can be sexy as well. Pupils of Chatham Grammar School for Girls in the 1950s delighted in wearing their hats cocked suggestively. When they also took to pulling down their stockings, the effect must have roused many local boys.

In fact, altogether, school headgear has traditionally been treated with disrespect. Girls of St. John's Convent, Abbey Wood, in the 1950s went so far as to rechristen their maroon felt hats 'pudding basins', then, still more appropriately, 'po-pots'!

Pupils even at the posh St. Paul's Girls' School in the 1880s resented the bowler hat for being both unfashionable and ugly. Indeed one St Paul's girl who was sent to the High Mistress for wearing the bowler on the back of her head, rather than pulled over the forehead, has testified as follows:

> Most of the girls of fifteen and over, hated it as it was such an awkward shape. They dented the crown, curled the brim, and did everything they could to make it more fashionable.

The biggest curse of many schoolchildren has been the boater, referred to earlier in this book. Children have frequently had their boaters knocked off their heads by local boys, when travelling to and from school. One boy of Kent College in the 1970s who had suffered from this was so relieved when boaters were made no longer compulsory that he gleefully burnt his.

Prior to this period, the only relief afforded to Kent College pupils was the last Sunday of the term, known as Bash Street Sunday, on which boys bashed each other's straw hats, often until they were wrecked.

As a variation on the theme, boys of Rodbourne College, Bucks (1960s) used to visit Northampton, where they would send their boaters skimming under a moving bus, aiming for them to emerge intact on the other side. In this endeavour, they were painstakingly imitating Odd Job, in *Goldfinger* the popular James Bond movie, who threw his steel-rimmed bowler hat at targeted victims, killing them as soon as it struck.

There were less flamboyant ways of ruining boaters. One pupil of Chatham Grammar School for Girls gradually made hers unwearable by keeping it screwed up in her shoebag.

Boys of The Royal Hospital School, Ipswich 1932, departing on their annual Christmas leave in the standard naval uniform.

Girls of Red Maids' School, Bristol, 1980s, dressed in their traditional red and white.

Pupils enjoying a butterfly hunt on a summer's afternoon at Bedales School, 1900. Note the broad-rimmed sunhats and boaters.

Two boys at Harrow School, 1980s.

If boaters caused children trouble, they were also sometimes a public menace. In the early part of this century particularly, school children were keen to keep their straw hats low over the foreheads, in order to prove that they were upper class, but this blocked their vision. One Downside boy so hatted, knocked off a man's glasses with the brim of his hat while he was boarding a bus. The bus conductor remarked sagely: 'Doomed race, that's what we'd be, if everyone in England 'ad storrats.'

Even if worn correctly, the Downside boaters were precarious. As they were not made to measure, they rattled on boys' heads, and cords to prevent them from wandering, although offered to the boys, were too obtrusive to be popular. Most Downside pupils either stuffed paper inside the boater to keep it on their heads, or, still more frequently, would carry the hats, chewing on the straw, just as their boaterless contemporaries might chew on blades of grass.

Top hats in contrast were both popular and prestigious; indeed to be seen without one in public was, up to the start of the First World War, unthinkable. Highgate School in the 1900s, for instance, insisted that school staff and pupils wore top hats for the annual Sports Day, regarding failure to do so as a social indiscretion.

Indeed, from the 1950s, the top hat was so important to the up and coming schoolboy, that certain manufacturers made papier-mache toppers for boys whose parents could not afford the genuine article.

The top hat has always had its extracurricular uses. Pupils of King's College Choir School, for instance, enjoy pulling top hats over their faces, thereby concealing their identity as a prank. More lucrative, however, would be exploitation of the value placed on Etonian toppers, for instance, by tourists. One small Etonian, offered £5 for his top hat by a tourist, would have loved to have accepted but refused, too gauche to risk being caught in the street without his hat. Particularly commonplace was the use of toppers for storage purposes. An old Harrovian comments:

> The most valuable single thing I learned at Harrow came from a remark Bowen made to the form, "If you want not to forget a thing put it in your hat." It has been useful to me for over 60 years.

The top hat's popularity has been reflected in period literature. Lord Snooty of *The Beano* is a familiar figure with his top hat, and so is the respectable if pompous Arthur Augustus D'Arcy with his silk topper, the creation of the Amalgamated Press which was particularly known for the *Billy Bunter* stories.

The topper has survived so long, according to the Freudian School, for its phallic symbolism, making wearers feel extra virile. Further, James Laver, the celebrated costume historian, has offered this ingenious theory for its popularity in the days of industrial advancement:

> Many of the proudest wearers of top hats were men who detested industrialisation, and all its works, but they were compelled to adopt the symbolism of its chimneys, as it were, in spite of themselves, by the play of forces beyond their control.

Naturally, in the course of its long life, the schoolboy's topper has had its detractors. The raising of the top hat, according to Flugel, represents a symbolic self-castration, but this of course goes hand-in-hand with the aforementioned Freudian theory on the subject, which has a more positive note to it.

More real to schoolchildren is when local kids have thrown stones at their toppers, as at Wellingborough School in the 1890s. A former pupil there recalls how when he went to church in his top hat, stones 'pinged' and 'ricochetted' off its surface. Boys can furthermore be teased for wearing toppers, and Compton Mackenzie has stated that the Sunday top hat at St. Paul's Boys' School was a constant object of derision.

The top hat has lingered in some schools long after its time of high fashion, and is still worn in some, particularly choir schools, today. Its use was abolished in famous public schools such as Winchester, and decades later, Highgate then Westminster, due to its high cost. It was allegedly phased out at Eton because boys became increasingly reluctant to leave it outside chapel where it could not be easily distinguished from all the others.

Other headgear has never been treated with the reverence the top hat has commanded. The unhappiest kind of hat has frequently been the schoolgirl's beret, and pupils of St. Anne's Convent, Ealing have been known to pull the tassels off their red berets, chucking them out of the classroom windows at innocent passers-by.

Gosling max, ma, mi, min and quint, five brothers who were at Eton together, 1888.

Pupils of the various grammar schools in Kent have traditionally pitched their caps in the river, usually but not invariably after they have left school. This obviously shows what they thought of their uniform.

Vocal chords alone can, by one account, be enough to ruin headgear. An old Harrovian reminisces on the fate of the boys' hats at Lords:

> We chaff and holloa with the loudest, till we are black in the face, and hoarse in the throat with our exertions and find our hat reduced to the consistence and shape of a jelly, owing to the frequent rounds of applause bestowed on it.

The uglier the hat, the more severe is usually its fate at the hands of resentful schoolchildren. For instance, pupils of Christ's Hospital in the sixteenth century so resented their ugly red caps which were too small and slipped off, that they used them to scoop water from the pump.

Children's caps have been made still more ugly by experiments that had insufficient regard for children's dignity. Girls of Christ's Hospital School in the 1920s wore frightful caps knitted by themselves out of thick red rug wool. A former pupil recalls how 'awful' these were, how 'misshapen'. The alternative headgear available to pupils there was an extraordinary navy blue cap with yellow piping and buttons which the school chaplain gravely christened: 'The great panjandrum himself with a little yellow button on top'.

Amongst peculiar caps which came and went like express trains was the infamous telegraph boy's cap introduced by the Prince Consort into the uniform of Wellington College during the nineteenth century. There was also the eccentric pill box hat, brought into Colston's uniform, and the thick brown cap introduced into Emanuel School in 1746 in order to identify the pupils as paupers.

Children have fought for the kind of caps which have appealed to them. Rebels of Whitgift School in the Victorian era insisted on wearing especially floppy caps, trying without success to make them acceptable by putting the school badge on them. Gradually the cheap hardwearing and foldable cricket cap became adopted in schools, largely because it was acceptable to the wearers.

Pupils have had a respite from caps when travelling to or from school, when at one stage it was more acceptable to wear a bowler. In school most pupils have resigned themselves to wearing caps, although it has been hardest for the new boy. Writer Ernest Raymond here recounts a first capwearing experience at St Paul's Boys' School: 'It reclined uneasily on a head as full of funk as an apple on a pith.'

The cap becomes more acceptable if it is subjected to cheeky competition as in the case outlined by a correspondent to the Eastbourne College Magazine of 1874, in which some local poor children had the nerve to wear the Eastbourne College caps, personalised with their own white stripes.

On such occasions, the cap's tradition is evoked, and its pedigree is jealously safeguarded. One pedigree guarded particularly closely was the red feather in the caps worn by Girls at Sir John Cass School, the red symbolising the blood of the school's founder on his deathbed, significantly while he was writing his will.

Boys of King Edward VI School, Southampton, 1880, gathering round the maypole in their mortar boards.

One popular use for caps is to throw them up into the air. One boy who did this at St. Benedict's, Ealing, saw his cap carried away on a milk float, but he didn't care. Many children will play cap rugby or cap football, uncaring of their cap's fate, indeed often hoping it will be ruined. Likewise caps will be used as collecting bags and have been known to break under the strain of it.

It seems that children are unconsciously driven to destroy their caps, and this has never been more apparent as when boys lose them. One Downside boy went home for his holidays, having left his cap behind, and cousins who met him on the platform screamed, 'Where's your hat?' When he got to his house, his father's first words were: 'My God. He's forgotten his hat.'

Pupils of Malvern College had an opportunity to discard their caps when they took them off before the statue of St George, as they were obliged to do. More tantalising, however, because it never materialised, was the tradition at Blundell's School that if the founder's stone should break from flooding, boys would be allowed to 'toss their caps to the black-beamed roof'.

Popular at almost any school would have been the tradition at nineteenth century Westminster School that to wear a cap was a cheek, which led to its new boys throwing their school caps away.

Caps have been at their most popular when they have been coloured to represent a school team, and even then many pupils have been distinctly unappreciative of them. However, amongst sports enthusiasts within schools, these specialist caps have proved so popular that in the nineteenth century, for instance, they were granted a place of honour over the study fireplace when not being worn on the field of play. Amongst such caps were picturesque pioneers like the striped pillbox of the Harrow Football XI, or the fez, i.e. a skull cap or peaked cap which was popular in a number of schools.

Otherwise, caps have been popular amongst nostalgic old boys who may have hated them at the time they had to wear them. Compton Mackenzie here fondly recalls:

> We still sported the old red Maltese Cross on caps frayed or stained by three years or more of school existence and were extremely proud of them.

One doctor of the author's acquaintance had similarly fond recall of his old school cap, to such an extent that he has handed it down to his offspring, who attends his father's prep. school. In the course of 30 years, the cap has remained unchanged.

Likewise, old boys of Christ's Hospital, who carried their caps screwed up in their pockets, now recall this item of uniform with an especial fondness.

Caps have by now almost been phased out, one Headteacher thinks due to the shortage of caps in the Second World War. No longer were children expected to raise their caps to adults, although in some schools they were expected to salute them instead, a custom which has now also been largely abolished.

The Rifle Volunteer Corps, Marlborough College, 1860, the year it was formed.

Paul Capra, proprietor of Caps restaurant at the Pembridge Court Hotel, Pembridge Gardens, London W2, amongst his unique collection of caps which adorn the restaurant walls.

Doubtless the fashion for long hair in the 1960s has also played its part in killing off the traditional cap.

In the few schools where caps survive, they are seen as a quaint item of school uniform, useful insofar as they keep children's heads warm and dry. Perhaps somewhere, some day, there will be a major revival.

Old boys all over England cherish their old school caps, but perhaps none quite as much as Paul Capra, proud owner of Caps, a delightful cellar bistro located in the tranquil basement of the Pembridge Court Hotel, a stone's throw from the bustle of Notting Hill Gate.

A panorama of colourful school caps in tastefully designed frames adorn the cosy brick walls of this gourmet's paradise. Bright scarlet, deep green, striped yellow, black and red, with criss crosses or Roman lettering, here is that first Prep School cap, those prestigious rugger and cricket colours.

Paul Capra, private collector and enthusiast, was nicknamed 'Caps' during his own school days at Beaumont College in the 1960s. Upon leaving school, he gleefully threw away his own cap, but to compensate for this he has now painstakingly accumulated a unique collection. Inside the restaurant, the real showpiece is the local Weatherby School cap, as worn by Prince William, prominently displayed in a cap-filled recess for private parties called The William Room.

Chapter 5

UNIFORM UNDER FIRE

In the earliest years, schoolchildren were unencumbered with official uniform, and yet despite this, dressed uniformly. The clothes children wore for school and for play showed no distinction, in terms of social class. As Tacitus said of Saxon schoolchildren, c.100 A.D.:

> In every house you may see little boys, sons of lords or peasants, equally ill-clad, lying about or playing among the cattle.

Styles gradually developed in socially distinctive channels, and from the early eighteenth century, schoolchildren, unless they were in charity dress, wore much what their parents did. Loose breeches with shoulder straps, worn over the vest, were a particular favourite, and perhaps the prototype for modern jeans and T-shirts.

Children were becoming better dressed. Schoolwear, as well as children's wear generally owes much to the championing of warm and light children's clothing by Edward Mulcaster, the respected head-master of Merchant Taylors' School.

The world famous Rousseau took up where Edward Mulcaster had left off. In the second half of the eighteenth century, arguing that children should be treated as individuals, not just as adults in the making, he made this proposition:

> The best plan is to keep children in frocks as long as possible, and then to provide them with loose clothes, without trying to define the shape which is only another way of distorting it.

As yet school uniform was largely undeveloped, then low necked muslin frocks and boys' skeleton suits made their debut on to the children's schoolwear scene. From around 1825, schoolwear became heavy and hot, leading to great resentment amongst children.

Indeed throughout the Victorian era, comfort and practicality were not priorities in children's schoolwear. The eminent historian, Elizabeth Ewing, has proposed that children, like furniture, were obliged to represent their parents' material prosperity through their appearance, which is why children and furniture alike were embellished with velvet and plush materials, with fringes and bobbles.

Typical of this period was the Fauntleroy suit which hampered boys in its effeminate velvet and lace, and the Kate Greenaway style, now adopted by Laura Ashley, which was denounced for its impracticality and datedness, despite its apparent innovation. Much of the drab uniform which followed these developments has been in fact a reaction against them.

The popular 'Wilwer' style, as supplied by Lewis's of Liverpool, a leading school outfitter.

Correctly feminine yet practical

The essential Twin Set

F311
F311. *On left*. This charming twin set is in pure wool. The jersey has short sleeves and both cardigan and jersey are fully fashioned. In delicate shades of pink, blue or yellow.

Chest (of girl)	24	26	28 ins.
Prices (the set)	**45/-**	**47/6**	**50/-**
Chest (of girl)	30	32	34 ins.
Prices (the set)	**52/6**	**55/-**	**57/6**

Swim Suits

Not illustrated

F588. All-wool swimsuits in the regulation style. Very hard wearing and well made. In navy or black. Chest (of girl):

26-28	30-34	36-38 ins.
11/6	**14/6**	**17/6**

G11
G893

Blazer and Shorts

G11. *On right, above.* An expertly tailored school blazer with deeply faced fronts. Made in a specially selected wool and cotton flannel to withstand really hard wear, yet giving an attractive 'handle' and appearance. In navy. Chest (of girl):

24-26	28-30	32-34	36-38 ins.
50/-	**57/6**	**65/-**	**72/6**

G893. Divided shorts in rayon Moygashel. The attractive cut provides full freedom of movement. In navy, grey or white. Waist sizes:

22-23	24-25	26-27	28-29	30 ins.
25/-	**27/-**	**29/-**	**31/-**	**33/-**

For the chemistry class

G499
G499. *On left*. Practical science overalls in strong and washable cotton. Cross-over style with tie-belt. Rubber buttons on cuffs. Deep turning on hem. 'Sanforised'-shrunk. In green or blue.

Lengths	30-33	36-40	42-44 ins.
Prices	**23/-**	**24/6**	**26/-**

POSTAL CUSTOMERS SHOULD READ THE SPECIAL NOTES ON PAGE 2

Daniel Neal's were prominent suppliers of school uniform. These pages are from their summer 1954 catalogue in the years before the firm was taken over by the John Lewis Partnership.

Our popular modern Gym Tunic

G943. *On right.* Made from all-wool serge that is soft-handling, yet hard-wearing and guaranteed fast colour. Perfectly cut, made and finished. Modern round-neck, flared style with zip side opening; concealed pocket in side of skirt and a lined back panel to prevent 'seating.' A 3-in. hem for lengthening and a clever $1\frac{1}{2}$-in. turning at the waist allow for extra bodice length and future adjustment of the waist line. In navy only. Note the very keen prices !

Lengths	24-26	28-30	32-34	36-38	40-42 ins.
Prices	**47/6**	**52/6**	**57/6**	**62/6**	**67/6**

G915. *Not illustrated.* The classic pleated style with square neck. In all-wool serge with self-lined yoke. Pocket in side seam. Has 3-in. hem and a $1\frac{1}{2}$-in. let-down at shoulder. Navy only.

Lengths	24-26	28-30	32-34	36-38	40-42 ins.
Prices	**45/-**	**52/6**	**60/-**	**67/6**	**75/-**

GRAND RAINCOATS
at economical prices !

G590. *On left.* A real triumph of quality and value. Tailored with great skill from a gaberdine cloth of selected Botany wool and pure Egyptian cotton. Proofed to withstand all but exceptional conditions. Fully lined with additional protective interlining at all vulnerable points. 'Captive' belt, 3-in. turnings to sleeves and hem. In navy.

G578. A serviceable and well-cut raincoat in union gaberdine. For the more slender budget. In navy. Lengths 24-26 28-30 32-34 36-38 40-42 44-46 ins.

G590	110/-	120/-	130/-	140/-	150/-	160/-
G578	77/6	87/6	97/6	107/6	117/6	127/6

Green and brown raincoats are also available in our showrooms.

School Blouses

F7. Clydella blouse. Washes and wears splendidly. Cream only. Chest (of girl) :

24	26	28	30	32	33	34	35	37 ins.
16/6	**17/6**	**18/6**	**19/6**	**20/6**	**21/6**	**22/6**	**23/6**	**24/6**

F20. Poplin blouse cut and tailored to perfection with close-fitting cuffs and a trim collar that 'stays put.' White only. Chest (of girl) :

24	26	28	30	32	34	36	38 ins.
14/6	**16/-**	**17/6**	**19/-**	**20/6**	**22/-**	**23/6**	**25/-**

Daniel Neal's THE YOUNG PEOPLE'S STORE

TELEGRAMS :- EDE, HOLBORN 0602 LONDON.   TELEPHONE :- HOLBORN 0602.
CABLEGRAMS :- EAGLEHAWK- LONDON.

EDE & RAVENSCROFT
FOUNDED IN THE REIGN OF WILLIAM & MARY 1689.

ROBE MAKERS & TAILORS
93 & 94 CHANCERY LANE LONDON
WC 2

BY APPOINTMENT

BY APPOINTMENT.

LAW WIGS.

TO HIS MAJESTY THE KING
H.M. THE QUEEN & H.M. QUEEN MARY.

LEVÉE SUITS.

CLERICAL. COURT. DIPLOMATIC & PRIVATE CLOTHES.

Peers, Bishops. Judges. Clergy. Kings Counsel, Barristers, Solicitors & Municipal Robes.

THE FIRM HAS BEEN THE RECOGNISED AUTHORITY UPON COURT DRESS AND ROBES FOR UPWARDS OF 200 YEARS.

D.C.Simpson Esq.,
The Master of the King's   Scholars,
Westminster School,
Whitbourne Court,.Worcester.

12th June, 1945.

Sir,

We thank you for your letter of the 9th inst. The material you have sent is quite suitable and the quantity would approximate to the number of gowns you require. Our only trouble is in the making: Owing to lack of workhands we are hundreds of gowns in arrears and we do not like to promise you any definite date for the delivery, but if you care to leave it to us we will do out utmost. It really depends whether we are able to obtain more workhands in the near future. We will keep Mr. Gerish's letter, pending your reply.

With regard to caps, the manufacture of these has been stopped during the war and until we are allowed to put new ones in hand we are afraid we can give no date whatever for delivery.

We are sorry this reply is somewhat unsatisfactory, but as we are sure you understand, we are quite helpless in the matter.

Assuring you of our best attention.

We are, Sir,
Your obedient Servants,

A wartime letter from Ede & Ravenscroft robe suppliers to the Master of the King's Scholars, Westminster School.

There was a brief craze for sailor suits, which served to remind the world that Britain was, after all, a great sea power. The tradition has survived in the UK's various nautical schools.

Then came the Second World War, during which efforts had to be made to preserve school uniform. Some schools continued, despite the Board of Education's protests, to have unrealistic expectations regarding school uniform. The historian Alice Guppy pinpoints here one extravagant list:

> One girls' private school insisted on four summer dresses, in addition to the basic uniform: printed shantung, gingham, navy shantung with lace collar, and speech day frock of cream shantung.

Retailers urged schools to retain their school uniforms, which would effect the most economical use of available materials and labour. They discouraged alterations in style, since these usually required extensive work, whose toll in time and expense school heads were slow to appreciate. The cost of reducing the size of the crown on the schoolgirl's hat, for example, was quite considerable.

In fact retailers came under a great deal of criticism from school heads who failed to appreciate that they might be recommending expensive extras to uniform only because they were cheaper in the long run. School heads instead presented snobbish and impractical designs for school uniform that retailers had tactfully to shelve.

Everybody, however, except perhaps the children, agreed that uniform had to be preserved. School heads endeavoured to retain high standards. Accordingly, girls in various state schools were forbidden to wear trousers, and if they did so, girls were banned from class. Eton College clung to its traditional Victorian dress although it permitted the wearing of navy velour overcoats when the standard black kind proved unavailable.

However, Eton College's uniform, like that of other schools, was feeling the strain. One small Etonian approached the Eton Dame, and demanded a new pair of trousers. He was one of three brothers, and said: 'You see, I have never yet had a new pair of my own.' She signed an order.

Given wartime stringencies in uniform, Etonians were encouraged to waste not, want not. During this period, all wore stiff white disposable ties, which were changed every day, and on one occasion they handed over a large quantity of old ties to a rag-and-bone man.

Head teachers eventually adapted to the uniform shortages and modified their clothing lists to a substantial but necessary extent. They did, however, make specific demands.

For instance, Tonbridge School, Kent, insisted that parents should 'ensure that boys are not allowed to think that they might be careless or exaggerated in their dress'. Wycliffe College expressed the hope that parents would 'fulfil the colour obligations'. Taunton School, Somerset, offered its boys the option of dispensing with spare suits.

Wrekin College invited parents to sell surplus uniform to the school's second-hand clothing shop. Eastbourne College asked that boys should

The Cadet Corps band at Worksop College, Notts, 1901.

wear a blue suit on Sundays, and should have two jackets and flannel trousers for weekdays. It also pointed out: 'For the time being all rules have been waived and quantity and kind are left to the discretion of the parents.'

Some schools had calculated adjustment to uniform regulations more fully. The King's School, Canterbury, listed the following items as 'not essential':

> 1 umbrella. 1 blue blazer or extra black jacket. 2 white gym vests. 2 pairs of white cotton shorts. 2 pairs of white flannel cricket trousers. 2 pairs of white socks.

Worksop College permitted the wearing of a dark Sunday suit, with long or short trousers as a substitute for school dress, with the wearing of shorts and soft white collars on Sundays. Dartmouth Naval College converted to dark shorts and knee length socks, while a few schools like The King's School, Bruton, reluctantly abolished weekday uniform altogether.

Many lists made concessions to shortages of mending materials. Felsted School stated:

> Mending wool is unprocurable in large quantities, and it will be of great help if parents will send one small skein of grey wool each term (and one of fawn if the boy is wearing the old uniform).

Abingdon School required parents to pin one loose clothing coupon to the clothes list each term to provide for mending. Furthermore, contributions of grey wool were 'gratefully received'.

Pupils of St. Paul's School, Barnes, evacuating London during the Second World War.

St. Paul's boys dressed for farm work during their wartime evacuation period in Berkshire.

Epsom College stated that parents would be charged if clothes had to be marked with a boy's name and number.

Parents and children alike were certainly feeling the pinch. It was in its way a watershed when one Peterborough Headteacher discovered that a pupil was actually wearing in the form of a dress some low quality print material given to her for sewing exercises. Desperate uniform shortages were already requiring desperate remedies, and the more enlightened schools were making open-ended concessions.

School staff were also hard hit, as some children discovered to their detriment. One teacher forced her pupils to wash and iron her personal underwear. The reason she gave them was the necessity engendered by the soap shortage. Naturally, however, the girls were smouldering with resentment, so the teacher had constantly to bully them into doing it, chanting: 'Rub the gussets, girls.'

Sadly but inevitably, uniform may have survived wartime stringencies, but fashion and aesthetic appeal went by the board. Under the circumstances, adolescent girls became all the more hungry to develop sex appeal through the way they wore their schoolwear.

A sense of let-down was quite usual. A former pupil of Chatham Grammar School for Girls reminisces: 'We should have worn tussore silk summer dresses - the fawn substitutes were ghastly.'

Another former pupil, however, claims greater satisfaction:

> Clothes rationing allowed us little scope for experimentation in personal attire, and as a change from the navy blue gymslip and white blouses of school uniform, padded-shouldered afternoon dresses and wedge-heeled shoes seemed the epitome of elegance.

Naturally children quarrelled over their uniform, all the more for its shortage. Etonians, for instance, dangerously delayed moving to the shelter during an air raid because they were squabbling over which items of unmarked clothing each could claim for his own.

Indeed, doing without uniform altogether was not unknown in wartime. One small Etonian was enjoying a bath when the siren sounded. He leapt naked out of the bath, singing: 'Cold and raw is the wind tonight, the bombs around us falling,' in parody of the old English song so beloved by the Eton choir which went: 'Cold and raw is the wind tonight, the snow around us falling.' Like a streaker, he ran helter-skelter for the shelter.

Doing totally without uniform did not necessarily involve nudity, and in some cases entailed wearing clothes tough enough for hard manual labour. For instance, the boys of St. Paul's, during the wartime evacuation period cycled, in casual dress, all the way from London to their temporary relocation site in Berkshire. They were put to hard graft as labourers on the surrounding farm, and wore rough tough clothing that was suited to this unscholarly purpose. For the first time, many of these privileged young men felt liberated.

Parents were always at hand to provide what clothes they could. When pupils of Highgate School were evacuated to Westward Ho, parents drove them to the site, with suitcases of spare clothes.

Spreading lime on the fields was the order of the day for the St. Paul's evacuees working here on the land during World War Two.

No uniform for pupils of Gerry Cottle's Circus School, whose classroom is a coach.

It is testimony to school uniform's great value to our society that it survived in such times of crisis. Much as some children loathed it, parents appreciated school uniform for its cost-effectiveness, and above all for its durability.

School uniform would not tear or break, wheatever vengeance children took on it. And take vengeance they did. They rolled in mud playing aircraft recognition games, and fell in dirt and slush while skipping with ropes to the tune of cheeky songs about Hitler and Churchill.

It was above all the role of spokesperson for children that Margaret Thatcher adopted upon opening the Junior Fashion Fair in 1959, when she advocated more attractive schoolwear.

What would not some children of the 1940s and 1950s have given to dress like some of today's children, who benefit from comparatively slack uniform regulations, or are even unfettered by uniform altogether?

The children who take real advantage of lack of uniform regulations are to be found in liberated comprehensive schools. Some, for instance, are still known to dress punk style in torn leather jackets embellished with messages of hate. Their dyed hair is spiked, and safety pins may hang from their ears like parodies of genuine jewellery. They wander through the corridors of certain comprehensive schools during weekdays, and sometimes down the King's Road at weekends. They have been known to shoplift. Their very demeanour conveys what Alison Lurie has interpreted as a 'demand for attention' and a 'cry of rage against those who should have paid attention to these kids in the past, but had not done so'. Their style of dressing is as drearily uniform as anything the strictest school imposes.

The leather jacket is worn uniformly by a far wider range of school-children than just the punks, and indeed sometimes by their teachers. As the leather jacket expert Mike Farren has pointed out: 'The leather jacket, in the eighties, still distinguishes between the streetwise and the wimp.'

Likewise, the popularity of blue jeans amongst the uniformless school crowd is high. To wear jeans is to be streetwise. What schoolchild would not wish this upon himself? It is also a symptom of the herd instinct. Jeans wearers have something fundamental in common, an attitude that goes hand in hand with the lookalike appearance.

While these and other children not wearing uniform at comprehensives like Holland Park School are likely to look scruffy, at some of the better private schools, they look like young gentry. Girls of Queen's College, London, for instance, while strolling down Harley Street, appear both cosmopolitan and sophisticated in long, heavy, quality skirts and crinkled blouses. Bags slung over shoulders bulge with schoolbooks, and their high heels clack on the pavements like castanets. Many are better dressed than their teachers.

Pupils of St. Paul's Girls' School, West London, are more likely to wear jeans, albeit fashionably tight and of an expensively cut kind. One St. Paul's girl chalked: 'Mr. X (a form teacher) is groovy' on her jeans. She was sent home for her cheek, but doubtless the teacher, unmarried as he was, was quite flattered.

Boys and girls of Bedales School, Petersfield, 1952, en route to class.

Straphanging on the Underground to school, older girls of Queen's College and of St. Paul's alike attract interested glances from older men as well as from schoolboys commuting. The same to a lesser extent is true for girls of Francis Holland School, looking drab but respectable and tidy in their maroon and grey mix.

Older boys too, at private schools like Ampleforth College, where they sometimes dress with startling casualness, attract interested glances from girls that pass their way.

Lack of uniform is only resented when the other children all have it. Here again is the herd instinct in action. Peregrine Worsthorne, for instance, recalls his early days at Abinger Hill School, when he did not yet have his uniform: 'I went about looking conspicuous, which is the last thing a little boy wants.'

As a general rule, the only time children wish to stand out from the crowd, sartorially speaking, is when they belong to a racial minority group that must safeguard its own rules.

For instance, Bradford schoolchildren may wear traditional dress, provided it is in the school dress, and religious jewellery, provided it is removed for PE lessons or for other physical activities. One critic has remarked that religious sensibilities are granted unfair precedence over other kinds of sensibility.

Boys and girls alike not wearing uniforms in schools whether private or state, which do not demand it, have something in common. They are all cool, so relaxed. But is this a good preparation for the stresses of adult life?

Chapter 6

UNMENTIONABLE UNIFORM:
UNDERWEAR AND NIGHTCLOTHES

Unmentionable uniform, otherwise known as school underwear, has a tradition dating back to the origin of mankind. Pupils of Ancient Greece wore loin cloths drawn up between their legs as underpants, while the teenage girls bound linen or leather girdles round their waists; Aristophanes and Lucan called them 'breast bands'.

The schoolgirl in the centuries that followed, became gradually more encumbered underneath. Up to the sixteenth century, she wore underpetticoats, which then gave way to the farthingale, a hooped petticoat covered with lavish and expensive material, which served the purpose of supporting her expansive skirt.

Any little girl of the era was to be seen and not heard and, almost incredibly, had to be gagged so she could not speak. This gag was, however, sometimes removed at school.

Release came at night. Schoolchildren in the seventeenth century would go to bed naked, a practice which was to persist for decades. The famous diarist Parson Woodford would sometimes 'get out of bed naked twice or thrice' to silence the dog, but such tasks more often fell on children.

Boys' underwear in the seventeenth century was not uncomfortable, particularly for the upper class boy whose drawers were invariably manufactured out of fine linen or holland. Wool was at this early stage avoided as it harboured dirt, and boys then were, by today's standards, excessively dirty.

The schoolgirl, who was more encumbered, wore a leather or whalebone bodice, just like her mother, and stiffened underpetticoats, but no longer the short-lived farthingale.

Not until the eighteenth century did the schoolgirl really feel confined by her underclothes. In this era, as soon as she was ten years old she was forced to wear stays which really squeezed her. One lady describes here what it had felt like:

> I was stood on the window seat whilst a man measured me for the machine, which in consideration of my youth was only to be what was called half-boned, that is, instead of having the bones placed as close as they could be, an interval... was left between each. Notwithstanding, the first day of wearing them was very nearly purgatory.

Some girls rebelled against underwear as restrictive as this, in a manner considered obscene at the time. Here is Princess Charlotte under inquisition: Lady de Clifford said, "My dear Charlotte, you show your drawers." "I never do but where I can put myself at ease." "Yes, my dear, when you get in or out of a carriage." "I don't care if I do."

Most welcome in contrast was the nightshirt worn by boys in the early nineteenth century, not just to keep them warm, but also to protect bedclothes from unwashed hair and bodies. Significantly at the Charity Hospital, Bedford, pillows were greasy because nightcaps were forbidden.

Pyjamas came into use towards the end of the nineteenth century, proving better ventilated and less cumbersome than the erstwhile nightshirt, and so rapidly superseding it.

At this stage, on the recommendation of the National Dress Society, wool was considered the most appropriate material for school under-wear. Also girls were squeezed into corsets that became increasingly restrictive as the poor creatures grew up. Adolescents humping about steel or whalebone framed contraptions, under several layers of petticoats, chemise, miniature crinoline, and skirts may be forgiven for feeling a little cheesed off. Finally, they were of course faced with a confusion of buttons.

Many schoolgirls gained hunches, and their back muscles wasted, while they became prone to fainting and sickness. Maternal opinion of the time remained nonetheless constantly severe. Some mothers insisted that their daughters slept in their stays, which one argued: 'Carry no hardship beyond an occasional fainting fit.'

Liberationists however made their case heard. *The Dictionary of Daily Wants* (1861) for instance stated: 'For the girl stays and corsets of all kinds must be forbidden during the whole period of childhood.'

Combinations, the ancestors of knickers and knickerlinings, once defined as 'chemise and drawers in one' were introduced in 1877. Girls of Christ's Hospital wore these throughout the First World War, using old sets as cleaning rags. A former pupil recalls: 'I had to put on combinations made of prickly natural wool; they were long-legged, and long-sleeved, and horrible.'

Corsets too have lasted into the 20th century and can be unexpectedly useful, as to the enormously fat pupil of Roedean School described here as changing into her coat and skirt on Sunday:

> The only way Marjorie could get into hers, was to wear a very heavy corset. She would get into it, tie the strings round the bed rail, and walk away until it was as tight as she could bear it. One of us had to take the strings off the bedrail and tie it up to her corsets for her.

This was of course highly embarrassing for Marjorie, given the taboo status of school underwear. Efforts to retain modesty were sometimes extreme, as recalled here by a former pupil of St. Paul's Girls' School (c.1916): 'If one girl climbed the ropes during gym, two others had to accompany her to hold down her skirt.'

Even the word knickers was taboo. At Christ's Hospital, girls were made to call knickers 'garments' or 'whites'. These euphemisms helped to draw attention to them.

Bras too were unmentionable and convent schoolgirls were ushered furtively into town by nuns to be fitted with first bras. Naturally in such establishments, bras became an overwhelming obsession with the pupils.

Efforts to retain cleanliness were taken to ridiculous lengths. Schoolgirls in the 1930s were often forced to sew studs into their blouses, to protect against dirty necks and smelly armpits. Would it not have been more productive to improve laundry and washing facilities? School needlework, never popular, became by this stage anathema to many schoolgirls.

Girls will of course be girls, and they seized their opportunities, especially during the Second World War. The younger girls at Holy Child Convent, St. Leonards-on-Sea, took to doing cartwheels across the lawn so their French knickers showed. The nuns promptly banned French knickers.

Likewise girls attending the school dance at another school were forbidden to wear black knickers. The Headmistress who made this ban was thus courting reaction. Schoolgirls by this stage were feeling it was their right to choose what they wore underneath. Indeed, during needlework classes at Holy Child Convent, St. Leonards-on-Sea (1940s), where pupils were making pink bloomers for the poor, one girl obtained permission from the supervising nun to keep her own effort since she was short of personal underwear.

Pupils' self-assertion in terms of underwear could be altogether more romantic. Many girls were in the habit of tucking handkerchiefs into knickers and storing loveletters in gymknicker pockets. Still more imaginative was the improvisation recalled here by a former pupil of Roedean School (1940s):

> Ros and I had cut two bust bodices, the official term for bras, from the blackout, having read with admiration the chapter in *Gone With The Wind* where Scarlett O'Hara cannibalises the curtains. It did not, in the thrill of the idea, occur to us that, when the light was switched on, two illuminated busts would signal cheerily to Hitler's hordes. Dame Emmeline, whose oration on the occasion of two gels being seen eating chips in Keswick is still spoken of in the same breath as Cato on Cataline, spat on her hands and delivered herself at some length on giving comfort and support to the enemy. Two small and suggestible juniors, with no busts at all, burst into passionate tears.

Underwear remained subject to discretion, particularly in the more conservative schools. At Oxford Girls' Central School, girls who went to dances had elastic threaded through the legs of their white lace-edged knickers.

In a similar spirit, convents, even in the 1950s, ruled that skirt hems should be no more than a specified number of inches from floor level as girls knelt at school assemblies. In reaction against this, many convent girls hitched up their skirts and tucked them into their knickers, so they could run around unencumbered, whenever they were not being supervised, and sometimes too when going to and from school.

Occasionally underwear liberation was encouraged within schools. Girls of Virgo Fidelis, London (1960s) were allowed to play badminton in their knickers. More daringly, boys and girls partaking in music and drama lessons organised by the alternative comedian Ivor Cutler at The

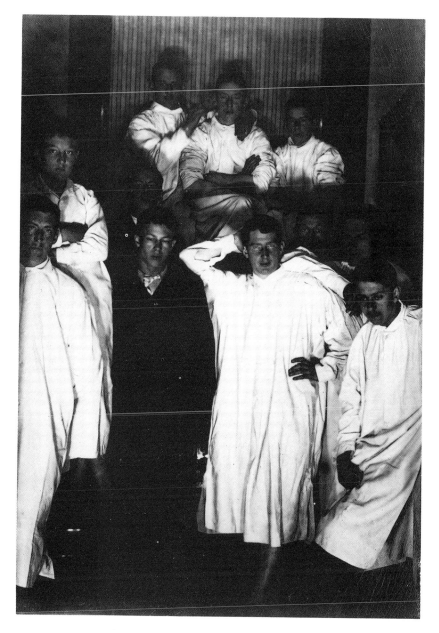

Bedtime for the boys of Merchiston Castle School, Edinburgh, 1888. Note the long nightshirts.

Ready for bed at Rydal School, N. Wales, 1940.

Fox Primary School, would run around in underclothes, sometimes showing parts of their bottoms for instance.

Nowadays underwear, unmentionable as it is, is a vital part of school uniform, and vividly recalled by all. It remains of course a source of furtive interest in children, still giving rise to salacious ditties. It is still not uncommon to hear in the prep school playground this oldie: 'Ladies and gentlemen, take my advice. Pull down your panties and slide on the ice.' Another oldie affording a new generation of girls a bundle of giggles is: 'You can't get to heaven on a Playtex bra, 'cause a Playtex bra won't stretch that far.' Sexual and lavatorial intrigues become muddled together in children's minds, and are often both linked to school underwear.

Many prep school boarders, for instance, have hardened themselves to rituals in which pants and shirt are interchanged with pyjamas at the precise psychological moment which allows minimum exposure to the wearer's private parts.

At such times boarders see their underpants on show. It is no wonder that they choose to wear brightly coloured pants, often red or purple, rather than the old-fashioned cream or white which not only is more translucent but also shows embarrassing stains.

Gaudy underpants are worth parading in the dormitory before lights out. Prep school boys are proud of their underwear, and all try to wear the same favourite colours.

Even when in bed, they must in some schools be fashion-conscious. One prep school Headmaster, just before turning out the dormitory lights, bent over one bed and undid the top button of the occupant's pyjama top. 'Be sporting,' he said.

Clearly then school underwear, like other school uniform, has to conform to the norm, in name as well as in kind. Significantly, a former pupil of Roedean School here recalls:

> On the first day of each term we each had to go through the contents of our trunks with Matron, and I was in trouble at once. Mother had filled in the required list, starting with '6 singlets' – What on earth does that mean? said the surprised matron, and we had a confused conversation until she gathered that I came from some primitive country (called America) where they did not know a vest by its right name. Worse was to come over what the English called a liberty bodice.

Underwear certainly has its pride of place in the school uniform repertoire, and it is hard to take seriously the suggestion from one learned quarter that it is becoming redundant. Without underwear, our children would be cold, and terrified of being seen in their naked state whenever they undressed.

Chapter 7

SPECIAL UNIFORMS,
AND ORDINARY UNIFORMS ON CEREMONY

Ceremony is all important in schools, evidence of how concerned they are with externals. School uniform has to be spick and span to impress all onlookers. The commitment to this requirement in schools can assume almost pathological proportions.

In particular, members of the school cadet corps must look particularly impressive for external inspections, the standards of which are dauntingly high. This can cause the boys real anxieties. One small Etonian rushed into the Dame's room with a bundle of cadet corps clothes in his arms, babbling:

> I have got to be on parade in two minutes, and they seem to have made me a lance-something, and I have got to wear this – I don't know where it goes...

Some boys of course are worried for weeks by the high standards required for looming cadet corps inspections. One junior boy strapped a handkerchief over his head every night for weeks to flatten his hair in preparation for the centenary inspection of the Downside Cadet Corps in summer 1914. He talked about it constantly in his sleep. The subsequent parade prompted Colonel Gasquet to remark sarcastically: 'They look quite ready to receive the Germans.' His attitude was much resented.

More flattering was this judgement on the turn-out of an early Cadet Corps at Rugby School. Lieutenant-Colonel W.P. Scott said: 'I consider that the condition of the boys' boots would have been a credit to any unit of the army.'

Indeed the dress of schoolboy cadets has been known to impress ordinary soldiers too. One cadet of Giggleswick School (1914), which has been renowned for the strength of its CCF, was once stopped in the street by two soldiers who asked him where they could obtain the marvellous non-metal buttons on his cadet uniform. Such buttons never needed polishing, and it is this which they had cottoned on to.

For every person who admires school cadet corps uniform, there are a hundred who will pillory it. Cadets of Emanuel School (1909) became the laughing stock of the rest at CCF camp, due to their eccentric bright red and drab grey dress. Cadets of other schools quipped: 'If this is their service uniform, what must their full dress be like?'

Since involvement in the cadet corps has been compulsory in many schools, there have been umpteen critics and rebels from within the system. Some cadets of Giggleswick School, for instance, have worn pyjamas under their breeches, and school shirts beneath their tunics,

A volunteer of the Rugby School Corps, 1860, to which a cadet division was added in 1873. The grey uniform was typical of rifle volunteer units of the period.

Cadets on parade at Marlborough College, 1886.

The school band of Giggleswick School, Settle, 1979.

The Artillery Company, Eastbourne College, 1896.

The Duke of Connaught inspecting the St. Paul's Cadet Corps, 1919.

also covering beds with greatcoats on cold nights. Not infrequently, boys have planted turds in the boots of enemies or weaklings during those long nights camping out under shelter of bivouacs.

Occasionally natural disasters turn the smartest cadet corps uniform into an unimpressive sight. A former pupil of Downside (1920s) recals here the effect of a spot of rain:

> Caps, tunics, trousers, puttees not only got darker and darker in shade as the heavens brightened, but with the weight of water they had picked up, they became heavier as well. Like blotting paper, they were liable, while in this state and even when subsequently dried, to tear. Changing men's clothes after parade was, therefore, an exercise of some hazard: an impatient elbow might easily appear through the steaming sleeve, a too-active knee through the steaming leg of the trouser. And always there would be a brown-green stain on whatever lay underneath.

First year scholars of Westminster School still annually partake in a traditional obstacle race, which involves dodging past trees and under tennis nets in old scholars' gowns, mildewed and ragged from such usage in earlier years.

School uniform had traditionally stood on ceremony in great splendour during the Eton versus Harrow cricket match at Lords. A former pupil of nineteenth century Harrow here recalls how they had all dressed for the occasion:

> Morning dress was rigidly observed, with fancy silk waistcoats of wondrous hues, with resplendent topper, frequently of the grey variety and of course white spats, patent leathers, and yellow gloves.

Tail coats go to war, Eton College, 1939.

THE GREENWICH ROYAL NAVAL SCHOOL BOYS.

Designed & Lith.d by T. Clare 16 Frith Street Soho Sq.r

Inscribed

An Eton hunting group, 1910.

The band of George Heriot's School, 1900; some of the uniforms seemed to be a poor fit.

If possible still more picturesque was the garb in which Etonians would be attired for the glamorous and famous Montem ceremony. The boys would don military garments, and in asking the local population for funds to support their school head through Cambridge University, would be the fittest, best spoken, and above all most smartly dressed beggars in town. As one member of the public who also happened to be an old Etonian put it: 'I love to be asked for salt by a pretty boy in silk stockings and satin doublet.'

Just as eccentric and picturesque, albeit kept within the confines of the school, was the Harrovian football team's infamous 'inquisition'. In this ceremony, juniors stood trembling on tables before members of the Football Eleven who were clad in scarlet dressing gowns. The poor trembling wretches would have to answer sporty but pedantic questions such as: 'How many nails are allowed in boots?' and 'What is the last letter but fifteen in the rules?' Any victim who failed to answer correctly would suffer a 'progging' with toasting forks, and drinks of heavily salted water until he was sick.

Likewise, boys of nineteenth century Downside would playact in the amazing Boy Bishop tradition. Every Christmas, Downside boys would elect one of their number to be king, with licence to dress the part and to reign, with such courtiers as he appointed, over the school for a whole season. The king had the privilege and the duty of organising festivals for the local community at large, as well as for the school.

Not all ceremonies are so flattering for wearers of uniforms. Boys of Royal Russell School, for instance, kneeling in their nightshirts for morning prayers at the ungodly hour of 6.00 a.m. daily, were prone to catch cold.

Most humbling of all, however, was the regular uniform of strengthened linen smocks and blouses, with wooden clogs edged with iron, worn by pupils of the Friends' School, Great Ayton, for a full twenty years. This uniform was suitable for the manual labour which formed such a large part of their curriculum. The older children, if it wasn't for their brown Glengarry caps which they also used for cushions, would have been indistinguishable from local farm labourers.

It is rarely discomfort that has caused children to be ashamed of, or even to disown their school uniforms. Social stigma is the one major curse on any item of school wear, and is likely to cause its annihilation, unless of course a way round it is found. For instance, pupils of Camberwell Green Coat School were allowed to dye their uniform black as a reward for good behaviour, and they relished this because it rendered their charitable status unobservable.

Cadets of the naval schools take pride in their uniform whose colours were chosen by George II as a result of seeing the Duchess of Bedford riding through the park, in a fabulous blue and white habit.

Children confined to bona fide detention centres naturally resent their uniform the most, and at one Cleveland based institution leave their regulation black plimsolls positioned in the form of a V-sign on their beds.

Boys at The Royal Hospital School Ipswich swarming up the mast.

Remembrance Parade, the London Nautical School, 1980.

Sailor boys of Royal Hospital School, Ipswich, 1890s, dressed formally for assembly.

Boys of Westminster School, 1950, in their annual display of casual dress, scrambling for the prize pancake during the Shrove Tuesday 'Pancake Greaze'.

A bee-keeping class at James Allen's Girls' School, 1900s.

Etonians, happy to have dyed their old clothes black, supposedly in mourning for the death of George III who favoured Eton, have been less happy about the pre-war custom of removing gowns outside the prefect's study before entering for a beating.

Perplexed more than unhappy were girls of Christ's Hospital School when at about the same period, they were told to wear stockings over their boots, upon going out in the snow. A former pupil here speculates: 'Perhaps they just wanted to use up cupboards of old grey stockings which must have been in great danger in the way of moths.'

Naturally, the more eccentric and discomforting varieties of school uniform have become extinct. For example, the huge cushions called bot-pads which boys of Bishop's Stortford College used to bring into the classroom to make seating more comfortable were abolished in 1927, after they had been used too often as missiles. One parent mourned their demise, on grounds that these bot pads had saved wear and tear on the trousers.

Also extinct is the 'cock hat and show rag' dressing style, adopted on specified Sundays in the 1930s at Kent College, when pupils went to church with hats tilted, and with handkerchiefs drooping from pockets.

A few schools such as St. Leonard's, Fife, and Albyne School for Girls, Aberdeen, retain the kilt as compulsory dress. British-born teachers have always been the kilt's staunchest supporters, which says much about the British fixation on school uniform.

Played once and once only at Marlborough College was the shoe lace rope trick, when one Charles Diggle, at the turn of the century, pilfered laces from an assistant master, to stretch them across twenty feet of a classroom.

The traditions that have lasted usually serve a social purpose. Pupils have always dressed up to impress the opposite sex. A former pupil of Bradford Girls' Grammar School recalls her dressing to meet boys, in the course of a visit to Stratford:

> An excited bustle pervaded the dorms as we dressed for the evening. An hour later, we emerged like butterflies, in full evening regalia, having shed our denim chrysalises.

Prizegivings have always shown school uniform at its best, and will continue to do so. A former pupil of South Hampstead School here recalls one such occasion:

> I was lucky to be at school for the great Albert Hall Prizegiving of 1907, when Princess Louise gave the prizes. We all wore white with orange bows fastened to our chests, and I think my original bow and hat band are now in the school archives... We went to the Albert Hall in horse-drawn charabancs, and though I did not win a prize, I was in the school choir.

Still as welcome and as necessary a release as it ever was for boys of Westminster School is the Pancake Greaze held every Shrove Tuesday in which participants, dressed scruffily, perhaps with stockings over their heads, scramble and fight for the prize pancake. The winner of the 'guinea' awarded for securing the largest piece of pancake is likely to have thoroughly earned it, and to have torn his clothes in the process.

Queen Mary, accompanied by King George V and the Prince of Wales, awarding the first prize at the Westminster School 'Pancake Greaze', 1919.

Surviving by a hairbreadth, unnecessary as it may appear, is the incredible ritual sustained in the sixth form at St. Anne's Convent, Ealing. It still occurs annually, and the local police are always secretly forewarned. The girls sleep on the school premises all night, then dressed in pyjamas, dance a little jig at school assembly the next morning. The ritual is and always will be important to these brave schoolgirls. They have the nous occasionally to ridicule school uniform.

Chapter 8

THE TRADITION OF UNIFORM

Uniform traditions stem in large measure from those of the great public schools, and of Eton College and Harrow School in particular.

The Eton suit has earned its pride of place in the school uniform museum. It is a sober garment that has given rise to countless imitation models. One Eton housemaster considers that it was introduced to prevent 'individual eccentricities of the boys' dress', but this does not explain its colour.

A widespread theory is that it was adopted at Eton in mourning for the death of the crazed George III, who like Henry VI bestowed his favours upon Eton, sitting on the school wall like the boys and gossiping with them, asking gleefully after their floggings, as if he was a boy himself.

This theory has, sadly perhaps, been proved wrong through a manuscript by Edward Coleridge in the Eton library, which portrays boys wearing black five years before the death of George III.

Despite the fact that imposters to the Eton suit reared their ugly heads, Eton jealously retained the original item in its compulsory uniform lists, and the Eton authorities branded it with their name in reaction to the brazen competing styles emerging, such as the coatee.

Our foremost school uniform specialist, the Rev. Wallace Clare, has denounced innovations such as the coatee as slovenly, but he is attending to the aesthetic implications at the expense of the practical. Many innovative uniforms, broadly speaking in the style of the Eton suit, were extremely comfortable.

The original Eton collar proved so prestigious a garment that it eventually became worn by all classes of boy, featuring prominently in the Army & Navy store photographs of the 1890s. This collar was in essence an appendage to the Eton suit.

The Eton suit became the most popular outfit of the day, and Etonians of the Victorian era felt privileged to wear it, particularly at Lords matches, testing out its sex appeal on boys as well as on girls. What is more, this garment stayed in vogue, proving to be what the costume historian Elizabeth Ewing has called a 'prime example of a uniform being a fossilised fashion, as often happens in that area of dress'.

The Eton suit infiltrated the prestigious Harrow School, whose uniform tradition was less trendsetting than that of its major competitor.

Juniors at Harrow School wore short coats without tails which were sometimes called Eton jackets, although they differed slightly in that they were cut straight at the back.

Sunlight on the desks of boys working in Lower School, Eton College, 1935. Note the toppers on the window sill.

Pupils of Eton College, 1961, some still in short jackets, seated on Pop Wall on the Fourth of June, the only day lesser fry are allowed to sit there.

Harrow School insofar as its uniform was concerned aped the conservatism in fashion that characterised London Society, and condemned innovation in dress as swagger.

The Harrovian reformer had his work cut out for him, but managed nonetheless to find his way. A former pupil of the nineteenth century here recalls:

> When I was elected in 1873 to the (Harrow Philathletic) Club, I proposed that H.P.C. should be placed on the (club) cap to show what it was, as it was only a plain dark blue cap and easily confused with that of Winchester. But the school was very conservative and turned it down. However, the next year, I was tried for the school XI, and got my original motion carried by a large majority.

However, even abolition need not be permanent. For example, the original magenta and black of the Harrow football team, although abolished in the 1890s, were resurrected by determined old boys, and so enjoyed a new lease of life.

Unlike Eton, in terms of school uniform, Harrow was a follower and not a leader. Tailcoats, black waistcoats and toppers rendered older Harrovians virtually indistinguishable from young society gentlemen, until straw hats were introduced.

To offset its overall predictability, the Harrow School uniform has had its eccentricities. Dirty socks (1890s) was one, arising from the tradition that new Harrovians had to run on the grass in their socks, a compulsory exercise introduced to toughen them up. Another uniform quirk was the wearing of the Harrow fez (a flat tasselled games cap) at a tilt as a self-assertion ploy. An old Harrovian (1870s) recalled:

> I was known as 'the Shah' at Harrow and all my contemporaries still call me 'shah'. It arose from House singing on an evening when we all had to sing a song. The Shah of Persia had just made his first visit to England, and I sang a song which was popular then, 'Have you seen the Shah, boys?' and as I used to wear my footer fez on the back of my head and was dark, I was always called it.

Eccentricities pervaded school uniform generally throughout the nineteenth century. These were sometimes somewhat pointless except insofar as they stamped items of uniform with character and individuality. For example, the velvet skull cap with its gold or silver tassel that was awarded for achievement in the realm of sports at Rugby School, derived prestige in direct proportion to the extent of its shabbiness.

There was an equally quaint and futile tradition at Ipswich School, dating back to the Restoration period, that any boy not wearing an oak-apple, or at least an oak-leaf, on 29th May was pursued with stinging nettles. This tradition was to last right up until the 1950s.

Some eccentric traditions of the Victorian era had a distinct purpose. Boys of Forest School, Snaresbrook in the 1830s wore college caps from classroom to chapel, and this was supposed to be a sign of their respect for both their school, and their God. These college caps were what are nowadays known as mortar boards, an epithet considered vulgar at the time.

Of less abstract use was the practice at Sir Joseph Williamson's Mathematical School (1890s) of having 'pockets crammed with edibles'.

The Victorian traditions in school uniform have spread their influence into the twentieth century, in particular reflecting the Eton and Harrow trendsetting. At Harrow School, the blue blazer, grey flannels and brown shoes with straw hats became gradually converted from cricket dress to daily schoolwear, and eventually assumed the place of standard uniform in schools throughout the country.

Harrovian along with Etonian influence is prominent too in the Sunday dress at Shrewsbury School (1930s), which consisted of a morning suit, top hat, and vivid striped trousers, with a bumfreezer for the junior boy.

The senior boy of Shrewsbury School at least had no problem about keeping his schoolwear neat, smart and clean. All he had to do was to yell out 'doul' (stemming from the ancient Greek word *doulos*, meaning slave), and a fag would appear as if by magic, ready to polish his shoes or to brush down his blue serge suit, under threat of a savage beating if he failed to perform his task properly. Thus the senior boy was able to concentrate on what he was good at, namely posing, and a common method at Shrewsbury School in this era was to thrust hands leisurely in pockets, specifically while carrying schoolbooks under the arm.

Boys at other schools didn't always have such convenient arrangements for keeping their uniform looking clean. At Highgate School

King's School, Rochester Lower School, 1894. Note the lack of uniformity.

(1930s), for instance, the present archivist, Theodore Mallinson, confirms that boys' shirts stank from only being changed once a week, and that their collars were engrained with filth, despite which, incredibly, the Highgate matrons were grim bullies, insisting on unrealistic standards of cleanliness.

Rebellion against school uniform traditions was widespread in schools throughout the country at this time, and a particularly flamboyant example was when a girl at the Convent of Jesus and Mary High School, Felixstowe (1930s) climbed on to the dizzyingly high school roof, and stuck her dark velour hat onto the topmost chimney. For this heinous crime, the culprit was threatened with expulsion, and so won the unflagging support of the day girls whose contempt for the school uniform was unreserved. The boarders, however, more loyal to the system, ostracised her from that day.

The war period annihilated by necessity many picturesque uniform traditions such as that of Eton tailors wheeling made-to-measure suits in cars round the school premises. However, the green uniform at Cheltenham Ladies' College survived, although pupils were nicknamed the 'Peagreen Pantibrigade'. When pupils were housed in local accommodation during the Second World War, the Headmistress had to explain to suspicious American soldiers that the ladies in green were just schoolgirls, and not a fighting regiment.

In the practical 1950s, the panama hats with tight elastic straps that left pupils' necks so sore were abolished at a girls' grammar school in Nottingham, and in a number of other schools.

Into the swinging 1960s, hair was allowed to be worn long at schools like Bishop Vesey's Grammar School, where it had previously had to be cut short, in keeping with the emasculating image of the dull traditional uniform there.

Likewise at this period, girls of the progressive King Alfred's School were suddenly permitted to wear Marks & Spencers jeans and jerseys, a delightful experiment in liberalism which was never abused.

Conservatism in school uniform remains, as it always will, a powerful force, and sometimes won the day. At Sion Convent (1960s) it was, surprisingly, parents rather than the nuns who insisted on retaining the original blouses, as opposed to the modern drip dry alternatives, on grounds of their superior whiteness, even though they were lumbered with the extra ironing. Sion Convent has now closed down.

Nowadays, uniform traditions that have become entrenched with age would be most difficult to remove, given the numbers of former pupils and prominent personages who would resist it. For instance, the black tie remains compulsory wearing at Ampleforth College in sentimental commemoration of the accidental death of ten pupils while on a trip to York some time back.

More recent innovations can prove shortlived. Pupils of St. Theresa's School in Liverpool delighted in keeping their socks pulled down to their ankles until an embargo was placed on this practice by parents as well as teachers in the 1980s, to great effect.

The innovations that survive are generally of practical benefit, such as the introduction of the navy blue raincoat to replace the cumbersome Parka anorak. Sixth formers at schools like North London Collegiate School for Girls are often now exempted from the necessity to wear school uniform, so becoming endowed with the dignity inherent in freedom of choice.

Today's uniform is resented the most when it appears old fashioned. A recent former pupil of Harrogate Ladies' College recalls how pupils there resented the uniform as much for the ridiculous number of items required as for its offputting bottlegreen colour. She recalls being forced to wear there an old-fashioned gym tunic, knickers over her tights, and a V neck pullover, a cardigan, baggy 'gym jocks' resembling pantaloons for PE lessons, and heavy felt coats for chapel. Other compulsory items were tracksuits for running, mackintoshes and berets for Sunday walks.

All the schoolwear was green although none envied the brown and yellow worn by girls at the neighbouring Queen Ethelburga's School, which made them look like McDonald's Hamburgers on legs.

These days, when school uniform has come under attack, the old boys safeguard the items they had worn in their day, keeping them in old Gladstone bags, school hatboxes, and battered old tuckboxes. Where possible, they will hand down items of schoolwear and the receptacles that contain them to their sons and heirs.

Pupils who wear school uniform even nowadays feel pride in it, coupled with their resentment at its restraints. Tradition runs through their dress like the thread which keeps it together, and has retained its rightful status as the *sine qua non* of school uniform.

Chapter 9

CHILDREN'S ATTITUDES TO UNIFORM

School uniform most pleasing to adults may be anathema to the children who actually have to wear it. We are reminded that beauty is in the eye of the beholder.

The less elaborate the uniform children have to wear, the less fun they may be able to find wearing it in unofficial ways that pervert all it stands for. Children of Ancient Greece, for instance, who wore neither tie nor collar, were denied the pleasure of tieflicking. The same may be said of pupils of Loretto School, whose loose collars and lack of ties nonetheless helped cultivate in them a tough Scots image, doubtless a source of pride for some.

The elaborate and traditional uniform has been pilloried from time immemorial as a symbol of authority and institutionalism against which any pupil worth his salt will react. Even the renowned King's scholars of seventeenth century Westminster would not allow themselves to be confined by their gowns, as this surviving scrap of a period letter makes clear:

> The King's scholars (who 'tis thought are locked in)... have openly and commonly been seene in the daytime out of colledge, walking about without their gowns, drest up with swords, laced cravatts, and cravatt strings etc.

Uniform, if not removed in this manner, was during the period exploited to pupils' own ends. For example, a charity boy of seventeenth century Christ's Hospital once illicitly wrapped his lunch of boiled beef in his handkerchief, and put it in his pocket to take home to his starving parents.

In this and in countless other ways, children exploit the school uniform inflicted upon them. A particularly dramatic case of this emerges in a schoolboys' revolution at Winchester College (1818), in the course of which the rebels hung a symbolic red cap from the founder's tower. On this occasion, the army was called in to restore order.

At around this period, younger boys in the public schools were made to clean boots and clothes of the seniors, but the rebel's voice made itself heard in the Westminster School magazine for instance, through whose columns a contributor in 1829 proposed that blacking shoes under threat of a beating was 'slavery in man or boy'.

Schoolchildren of the nineteenth century, as to a lesser extent at other periods, were used to swaggering about with hands in their pockets, playing as if they owned the world.

In Draconian reaction to this, Montague Butler, the strict headmaster of nineteenth century Harrow ordered all his boys' pockets to be sewn up, and this was enacted ostensibly without protest. However, during the legendary Eton v. Harrow matches, Etonians sneered at Harrovians for unthinkingly trying to thrust their hands in their pockets. Butler immediately commanded that Harrovians' pockets should be reopened, so that the boys should not lose face before their formidable rivals.

When items of uniform are compulsory wearing in a school, they will invariably give rise to nicknames that demonstrate certainly an obsession with the dress as well as perhaps reverence for it, perhaps contempt, or most likely a bit of both. One old Harrovian of the nineteenth century here relates how one of his contemporaries there:

> ...had the nickname of 'Breeches', which was given him for the following silly reason; his name was Surtees; a friend of his one day familiarly called him 'Shirts', hearing which another boy remarked, how absurd to call him shirts! Why you might just as well call him 'breeches'; after which, sure enough, he was invariably called by that name, for which very few boys knew the reason, and being very popular he retained that name during all the time he remained at the school.

In schools like Eton and Harrow misuse of uniform, as of everything else, was enacted on a grander scale. Etonians of the nineteenth century who made use of their cloaks to conceal a sledge hammer they smuggled into their Headmaster's study, removing the offensive weapon once in there and smashing the place up, were expelled for this exploitation of school cloaks as much as for their act of vandalism.

Etonians in particular win uniform battles occasionally, and a prominent case in point was when after one nineteenth century master had formally abolished the tradition of boys wearing red after the splendiferous Montem procession, a far larger number than usual appeared so dressed. The master was scared by this, and wisely for his peace of mind, took the hint.

Likewise, boys at Beaumont staged a hat parade in the school playground in protest against a new regulation to the effect that they would have to wear hats at Lords. Most satisfyingly, the regulation was instantly abolished.

However children were not permitted to take their choice of dress style too far into their own hands, especially where it broke with tradition as during one Christmas at Emanuel School (1863), when two pupils dressed a colleague up in a Yorkshire girl's hat and cloak, and so disguised this pupil went to a nearby pub, bought some bottles of gin, and brought them back to school. All those involved in this conspiracy were exposed and expelled.

Pupils of Radley College (1860s) who hated their uniform took counsel from their master Mr. McClaren, who supervised them doing exercises of his own invention, which he claimed in a book published in 1869 would make them grow out of their uniform in a matter of weeks. His system too came into force at Marlborough College, but proved not efficacious although he made plenty of money out of his book.

Ugly school uniform can be made bearable by extra dress which, while not replacing it, mitigates its effect. For example, the charity pupils of Bell Lane School (1870s) insisted on wearing boots, as they could not bear wearing charity clothes.

Lounge Lizards, Marlborough College, 1870.

The introduction of extra schoolwear was not always necessary to enhance what was already being worn. Pockets have been a source of relief to the sartorially suppressed schoolchild throughout the ages, and have invariably been a primary inclusion in even the humblest school uniform.

Junior pupils at nineteenth century Westminster School for instance kept dips of ink in their breast pockets. This proved most useful, although they had problems keeping the sponge wet without inking their handkerchiefs.

The greatest relief pockets have afforded school children is doubtless in their use for practical jokes. The famous author to be, G.K. Chesterton, while daydreaming in between classes at St Paul's Boys' School, inadvertently had his pockets filled with ice. The jest, as described here, proved most entertaining for his classmates:

> When class reassembled, the snow began to melt, and pools to appear on the floor. A small boy raised his hand: Please Sir, I think the laboratory sink must be leaking again. The water is coming through and leaking all over Chesterton.

Pockets, here a source of embarrassment, may also be used to thwart it. Here is one case in point:

> The Headmaster of 'D' school frowns on boys who slough along with hands in pockets. On one occasion a boy caused him considerable surprise by running past him with his hands in his pockets. "Hands cold?" enquires the Headmaster. "No sir!" came the reply, "Belt's bust."

This shows how pupils would make the best use of their pockets, as did day boys of Emanual School who used them for smuggling in forbidden tuck. Girls at Sherborne School at this time used their knickers for the same purpose.

Generally, pupils around the turn of the century would make the best use of their uniform. The Radleian dandy, for instance, used to strut about squinting through his monocle, and shaking his walking stick eloquently, and he would periodically remove his cap whose lining was as colourful as its outer layer.

Etonians at this time would sometimes go too far, sporting white triangles, i.e. leaving shirts hanging out in an effort to appear supercool and casual. If a popper (members of Pop, Eton's elite body) witnessed this particular slovenliness, he fined the offender, saying '50p in my room by lock-up'. One such miscreant paid his fine by cheque, writing on the back of it: 'I've made it payable to Tap (i.e. the Eton College bar) because this is where it will be spent.' He earned himself a savage beating for this cheek.

Etonians would discard their uniform and dress like scarecrows at the annual 'Twit of the Year' contest, which was sanctioned by the authorities. In this ritual, local people would hurl rotten fruit at volunteer Etonian victims, and community relations through this apparent lowering of the class barriers were supposedly enhanced.

Some pupils, rather than thus seeking to be made a fool of, would go out of their way to impress, and in this tradition, the now distinguished Peregrine Worsthorne admits that as a boy at Stowe School he had dressed up in a cloak and floppy hat to make himself attractive to older boys.

All pupils, whether or not aiming to impress, will unconsciously or otherwise dress in a manner that reflects their personalities. An Eton housemaster puts it like this:

> A characteristic of adolescence is to want to proclaim individuality through the costume worn; it is a blameless form of existentialism.

Not uncommon is the following type of pupil, dressed here as Edward Blishen remembers him at the Vale Preparatory School:

> It was a fair guess that Stent Davis had rarely known a moment of emotional security. His clothes reflected his condition: everlastingly rumpled, torn.

In contrast, there is always what may be described as the institution-alised personality, who clutches at school uniform, cherishing it for its endowment of anonymity, its stamp of institutionalisation. As an old girl of Roedean School (1920s) puts it:

> To have everything specified from underclothes to the width of hair-ribbons was indeed a blessing. There is no greater freedom than waking up in the morning and knowing exactly what you are going to put on.

Indeed, for certain types of children, to wear uniform is to celebrate, and to deviate from the norm in this respect is a discomfort as well as a heresy. Two schoolchildren of the 1930s, for instance, dyed their stockings black so that these would be the same colour as everybody else's.

A pupil of Royal Hospital School Ipswich, 1860s, striking a casual pose.

Children who are forced to dress differently not by their own will may be rescued by teachers, natural guardians of institutionalised uniformity. A female pupil of Emanuel School, for instance, once appeared in school dressed in woollen garments, which her teacher immediately confiscated. Here is her retrospective laudation of the schoolmarm's action:

> We were not allowed to wear wraps of any kind, not even in the worst weather when we were out at play. However, it did not kill me, as my mother had predicted.

So loyal to their schoolwear do these sorts of pupils become that they don't know how to dress when off the school premises. Schoolboys in particular have their ideas about fashion formed by the prejudicial comments of the reactionary pipesmoking masters in tweed jackets or academic gowns who organise their lives. It is telling that when one boy decided to run away from Downside, the famous Catholic public school, he sent a note to another boy, inviting him up to the dormitory. The other boy arrived, and saw clothes arrayed on the bed. "I am... about to run away," said his companion. "You are, I understand, an authority on dress. Perhaps you would be so good as to tell me, quite frankly, what you think I ought to wear for this?"

Girls, more fashion conscious than boys, have been equally loyal to their uniforms and lost without them, even as they have detested them the more for their ugliness. For instance, pupils of Uplands School (1930s) wore black and white dresses, with coats to match, which bore a startling resemblance in colour combination to Woolworth's sponge-bags. When the poor creatures took their compulsory Sunday walks along the promenade, they were sneered at by the local boys, and, not surprisingly, some felt like stripping off altogether.

Nudity or any physical state approaching it is of course an ultimate rejection of uniform, and it is perhaps unconsciously for this cause that new boys at Kent College (1930s) were made to run the gauntlet between beds in the dormitory, while more seasoned pupils whipped them with knotted towels until they screamed, and eventually collapsed.

This ritual apart, pupils of Kent College in this era were fearful of authority that insisted they abided by school uniform regulations, and conscientiously played the game, despite any resulting discomfort that accrued to them. A former pupil of Kent College here recalls the agony of donning the compulsory white shirt and collar on Sundays:

> The combination of lost/broken/unmanageable collar studs with the misery of fly buttons (zips were never permitted) made Sunday mornings a nightmare. I never did master the collars and I have memories of whole days spent with the studs pressing into my neck; fortunately the rules were relaxed after a year or so.

Such agonies are part of the rituals of putting on school uniform and were in the 1930s manifold in schools throughout the country. Pupils of St. Paul's Boys' School, to take another example, detested the permanently made up ties some wore on grounds that they were infra dig, but the wearers, often due to their parents' whim, were forced to grin and bear it.

The apparently accepting uniform wearer might take out his resentment on his colleagues' dress, or maybe even on his teachers'. Here is an apology note penned by a pupil of Bishop's Stortford College earlier this century:

> Dear Mr. Alliot,
>
> I am sorry that I tied Mr. Morley's tails behind his chair. All I can say is that I did it in a moment of distraction – Your obedient pupil Jadd.

A less irreverent attitude towards school uniform, and an appreciation of its merits prevailed even amongst children around the time of the Second World War. Pupils of Radley College, temporarily donning old coats and boiler suits, secretly longed to be smartly clad in school uniform again.

Pupils still wearing school uniform clung to what they had. One pupil at Chatham Technical School stuffed cardboard in her leaking shoes, rewashed her one school dress every night, and continued to use a satchel that had become accidentally saturated with cod liver oil. She appeared however to the casual observer quite normally, smartly dressed, as was indeed her proud intention.

Children in the wartime era were sometimes deprived of underclothes, but did all they could to remedy this. For example, girls of one Nottingham grammar school, losing the suspender buttons of their liberty bodices, replaced them with sixpenny pieces.

Pride in school uniform was rapidly undermined by untimely innovations. When shorts were allotted to boys of Dauntsey's School, Wiltshire, this was ostensibly to break away from stuffy traditional dress, and, to considerable public amusement, masters wore them too. The scheme was doomed to ridicule from the start. Christopher Evans, the present headmaster, here reminisces:

> When a party of boys from Dauntsey's visited Oxford in the early 1950s, they were asked which Borstal they attended, and subsequently it was agreed that long trousers would be worn for official school outings.

Despite this, shorts worn on Dauntsey's School premises survived and prospered. Although these shorts were not always popular, appearing perhaps not manly enough, only rarely were boys exempted from having to wear them. Two such pupils in the 1960s were allowed to wear long trousers all the time, one because he had kidney trouble, the other because he had persuaded his psychoanalyst that wearing shorts made him feel conspicuous, despite the fact that four hundred boys were so dressed.

To avoid wearing compulsory items of school uniform of course needed special permission in school. Girls in many schools were supposed to wear gloves, for instance, and a pupil of Sacred Heart Convent Hammersmith was caught gloveless on the bus one morning by a teacher who proceeded to bawl at her: 'Get those gloves on immediately. You're a disgrace to the school.' Rebuke can however be as severe from contemporaries as from teachers, which writer Gerald Brenan found to his cost when he started out at Winton House prep. school with buttons on his shoes. The renowned novelist, Timothy Mo, similarly recalls here his days at prep. school in Finchley:

> I seemed to be different in so many ways. I wore funny Chinese army-boots above my ankles while all the other boys wore Clark's. I hated it.

Timothy Mo, now a publicly known figure, doubtless has every opportunity to speak out, as he did here, and headteachers who felt so inclined would of course have every opportunity to vindicate the dress regulations under which they had personally suffered by inflicting what dress regulations they chose in their own schools. The headmaster of the Oratory School, Reading, for example, abolished the white cricket blazer because it reminded him of the one he had worn in his own schooldays.

Generally, the 1960s was a time of liberation for the pupils. Some of the girls were wearing very short miniskirts in class, which prompted a sixth former debater to state: 'Miniskirts getting shorter is a sign that teenage morals are going downhill fast. We will soon reach bottom.'

So popular indeed were miniskirts that girls in convents who were not allowed to wear them rebelled. Pupils of one convent in the 1960s, emerging from the school gates at 4.00 p.m., stopped on the public road to roll up their skirts in the fashionable miniskirt style, much to the amazement of passing pedestrians.

The 1970s served to some extent as a reaction against all the liberalism, and during this era, the pupils of the better known feepaying schools in particular have sustained the most absurd uniform traditions.

Westminster School (1970s) was one of the very few even amongst public schools that proposed pupils should wear jackets unbuttoned, with flaps not stuffed inside pockets, and that they should thrust their hands in the pockets of their jacket rather than in those of their trousers. Few pupils, however, heeded this counsel seriously.

Less avoidable was the shapeless blue sack pupils of St Paul's Girls' School (1970s) had to wear for gym and lacrosse. The wearers found it barely covered their bottoms, and felt it furthermore made them look fat. All this was far less bearable than, for instance, the embarrassment experienced by sixth form girls at King's School, Rochester, in protecting their chests with steel saucers during fencing lessons.

In other schools, only some of the pupils felt insulted, while others felt uplifted by uniform regulations calculated to divide and rule. Girls of Harrogate School were awarded girdles for good deportment, and this aroused resentment amongst those who failed to win the prize, which culminated in successful moves towards vengeance. Girls, when first allowed into the sixth form at Wellington School, Somerset, were dressed more grimly than the boys, in grey skirts and blue blazers, and had to sit six inches apart from them during lessons. An old girl who had experienced this comments: 'It was unnatural, and I'd never inflict it on my own children.'

Nowadays as ever, children often appear protective, even proud of their school uniform, to the casual observer. This is particularly the case when they wear smart distinctive dress like the gold corduroy shorts worn at the preparatory school Felsted, concerning which the present headmaster, Mr. T.M. Andrews comments:

> Given the environment here, and the ease with which corduroy shorts can be

HRH Prince Charles hard at play, Hill House, Kensington, 1958.

Pupils of Hill House, Kensington, in their highly individualistic dress.

looked after, and the generally smart appearance that the boys have walking about the place, we will keep these for the foreseeable future.

A measure of the success of these golden corduroy shorts, and of the windcheaters that go with them, is the great extent to which they are worn by pupils during school holidays.

Just as popular are the unique rust coloured breeches and mustard jerseys worn by pupils of Hill House Preparatory School. However, a vast subculture incorporating school uniform exists in schools, which only the experienced eye can spot, although occasionally it is drawn to the public attention as when 650 pupils of a Hampstead comprehensive staged a sit-out in protest against their uniform. Amongst less openly displayed practices in coeducational schools is that of the boys tieflicking the girls, which has been standard at St. Teresa's, Liverpool.

In single sex schools, where sexual frustration festers, school uniform is deployed in children's efforts to discover their own identities. As a schoolmaster at Chatham Grammar School for Boys in the 1980s, the author has observed the following:

Boys tieflick each other, and use ties for fastening each other's legs in the changing rooms, for holding windows wide open, for makeshift armslings and guitar straps, for cleaning spectacles, and even as catapults. In drama lessons, ties are wrapped around the head for the Rambo image, or serve as lion-tamer's whips. After being misused in this way, they end up bedraggled and often partially unstitched.

Boys likewise exploit the rest of their uniform, using socks to keep banknotes in, and to shove up other boys' noses as a putrid joke. After playing a hard game of football, they wipe sweating faces on jerseys. They put on shirts back to front, so achieving their aim of looking like vicars with dog collars. They wipe chemicals spilt over the desk on their workshop aprons, sometimes wiping paintbrushes on their companion's apron when his head is turned.

Cleaning shoes by rubbing them on the backs of their trousers, these boys use them as makeshift rugby balls, to swat flies, and to prop doors open. They make conker strings out of their laces and, should they get the chance, will tie a victim's laces together so he trips.

Prior to playing football, Chatham Grammar School boys throw down blazers to serve as goal posts, afterwards picking them up dusty and trampled on. They pick off their blazer buttons to play tiddleywinks and will put them in the collection plate at Church services.

These boys cover the school badges on their blazers so as to avoid being ridiculed for them by children from the local secondary modern. The badge is in fact removable, and one boy wore his blazer without it quite passably at a registry office wedding.

An alternative emblem, perhaps of a favourite football team, is sometimes sewn on the inside pocket of the blazer. In the absence of towels after showers, the blazer finds extra service. Likewise the sleeves come in useful if boys have left their handkerchiefs behind, a shiny spot or two being the obvious giveaway sign.

Ties are not popular amongst these boys except for the purpose of 'peanutting', i.e. pulling a companion's tie down so hard that the knot tightens to a peanut shape.

In their leisure, Chatham Grammar School boys react vigorously against their standard black blazers and dark trousers, wearing what they judge fashionable. Baggy stonewashed jeans or Farah trousers rank high in their choice, together with Fred Perry, or Gallini T-shirts, and Gino Gapelli or Slazenger jumpers. They prefer white socks, trainers, and if their parents have the means and inclination, black leather jackets full of pockets, perhaps with a black leather tie and studded leather belt. Occasionally they will wear tracksuits too.

Conformity of dress, in or out of schools, need not, we must be thankful, lead to conformity of spirit.

Chapter 10

YOUNG LADIES AND GENTLEMEN

Ladies and gentlemen of every age, it may be argued, become defined by their dress. As in the outside world, so in miniature in schools. The top schools do all they can to make sure their pupils dress like young gentry. They would sometimes go to absurd lengths, in which context not unknown in the Victorian age was use of the blackboard. In his fictional masterpiece *Vanity Fair,* Thackeray here describes a regulation of Miss Pinkerton's Academy:

> A careful and undeviating use of the blackboard, for four hours daily during the next three years, is recommended to the acquirement of that dignified deportment and carriage so requisite for every young lady of fashion.

Another prerequisite of young ladies in the Victorian era was constantly, and not just when travelling to and from school, to wear gloves. A former pupil of St. Paul's Girls' School (1890s) recalls: 'If we were seen to arrive without gloves, we got an order mark.'

Young gentry's dress regulations were not necessarily reflective of academic performance, which had low priority in some schools. The Prince Consort introduced into nineteenth century Wellington College a military style uniform that was positively anti-academic, with its bright red cap, its green coat with brown buttons, and its flamboyant plaid jacket. This innovation delighted the school's founder who detested contemporary academic dress for its monastic influence.

The new Wellington College uniform was abolished after a particularly unflattering incident. An important visitor to the school, upon meeting the head boy at the station, had yelled at him 'Porter', thus prejudging him by his uniform.

Even the crudest uniforms in the public schools were not as obviously demeaning as the charity dress whose wearers were self-evidently then of a lower social class. Sometimes, the cruel distinction was made within the confines of one school. At Bromsgrove School in the nineteenth century, the private boarders wore white leather breeches, white socks, and black commoner's gowns in the style of Worcester College, Oxford, as well as cravats and mortar boards. How much more respectfully they were treated than the local 'scholarship' boys in the same school, known as 'blue chairs', who wore charity cassocks modified from the Christ's Hospital style.

Not that young gentry in schools had a particularly easy time of it, and part of their education involved learning to accept their dress. Thus it was that a pupil of King's School, Canterbury (1900s) who strode booted

The pinafore worn at St. Leonards-Mayfield School in the early 1900s. Note the striped stockings.

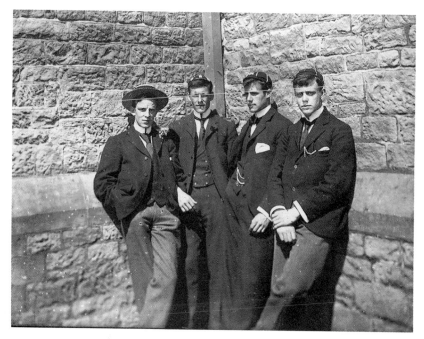

Seniors at Rossall School, Lancs, 1896. Note the buttonholes, watch chain and albert.

Boys at Rugby School, 1865, photographed by Lewis Carroll.

Two of the first foundationers at Wellington College.

The typically Victorian uniform at St. Mary's Hall, Brighton, 1880. This was also worn for hockey and tennis.

and spurred into the Cathedral was flogged for his pains. The King's School pupils generally had to have the sleeves of their gowns cut in this period, so that they would not harbour in them stones to throw at the local boys who taunted them.

Bullying from contemporaries was indeed more feared than punishment from teachers. Typical of practices in schools everywhere was that described at Uppingham by C.R. Nevinson in this extract from his autobiography *Paint and Prejudice*:

> The cricket eleven wore their white shoes, and any junior was captured, and bent over for their sport. They took running kicks at our posteriors, their white shoes marking the score, and a certain place counting as a bull.

By way of compensation, young gentry in schools had secret ways of exploiting their dress, and this too was their privilege. A former pupil of University College School, London (1900) here recalls a fellow pupil who had just pawned his best suit in order to back a favourite racehorse at the Derby:

> It lost, and when, later, I asked him how he was going to explain a missing suit to his mother, he replied that he had already acquired another just like it, from Harrod's, and charged it to his father's account there – no bother at all, because the family bought everything from that store, and the item would never be noticed.

Furthermore it was fun dressing up for occasions such as school dances, although, inevitably, there were restrictions. An old girl of Bradford Grammar School here recalls:

Working on the looms at Bedales School, Petersfield, 1906.

The cricket team at Durham School, 1930.

I enjoyed tremendously the winter of 1913-14, when I was first allowed to go to dances (never unescorted at first!)... Gentlemen wore white gloves to protect the ladies' dresses from the effects of a hot hand placed sedately in the middle of the back while dancing.

However pupils of the grammar schools would not wear the same quality of uniform as those in feepaying schools, and were not subject to so precise regulations on how to wear it. The blazer in the 1920s became everyday uniform in the grammar schools, whereas in the public schools it remained informal wear, an extra. Likewise in the grammar schools, the straw hat was in jeopardy due to the expense of retaining it, and for this reason at Sir Joseph Williamson's Mathematical School, Rochester (1930s) it almost died out. Obviously public schools such as Harrow have not had this problem.

Juniors at grammar schools in the 1930s would often stand uncorrected if they loafed about with their hands in their pockets, whereas this was frowned upon in the great public schools, and was punishable at Shrewsbury School by a prefects' beating. The wearing of popular 'Oxford bags' became frowned on in public schools, and George Smith, Headmaster of Dulwich College, once asked a pupil who was wearing them: 'What colour do you call your trousers? Would you say they are a crushed strawberry?'

Pupils in grammar schools valued their uniform more than those in feepaying schools, as their parents had often made more sacrifices to obtain it for them. A former pupil of one Nottingham Grammar School (1950s) was scared to get her gaberdine raincoat dirty, as this meant her father would beat her with a belt.

Class distinction, still defined by differences in schoolwear, is nowadays a source of irritation to some pupils of the great public schools... Times are unchanged since when Peregrine Worsthorne, being measured up for a knickerbocker suit at Stowe School, noticed: 'In no time at all there were a hundred ribald eyes glued to the window in menacing mockery.'

Boys of the King's School, Canterbury still sometimes surreptitiously discard their conspicuous black and white trousers, winged collars, and straw hats, in which dress they have been called 'penguins' by the local boys. There is a physical as well as mental relief in removing the frequently loose hats, the frequently chafing collars. Then they sneak into town to meet their girlfriends, often deliberately chosen because they hail from a lower social class. On these forays, their shirt tails hang out, and their trousers are a happy medium between flares and drainpipes.

Back in the dormitory at night, they throw varnished boaters at each other across the floor, thus showing a boyish contempt for their trappings of gentry. Perhaps their uniform is altogether too elaborate for this day and age.

Certainly, this criticism might be made of the uniform for Harrogate Ladies' College whose range is described elsewhere in this book. Suffice it to say that pupils there have treated their dress with contempt, tossing

Pupils of St. Leonards-Mayfield School, 1960s, wearing their unique cloaks.

Class ends at Harrow School.

Uniform at Gordonstoun School, Elgin, has a distinct Scottish flavour.

Radley College, 1986.

berets into the treetops during their Sunday walks, and scoring a bullseye if a beret settled high, and wasn't the girl's own.

The contempt has now spread to Harrow School, whose pupils look sometimes quite scruffy in blue blazers, carrying their straw hats in the hand maybe, or else forgetting to bring them altogether.

No longer do Harrovians submit to the absurd memory test once administered by senior boys on how many buttons they may wear undone at what stage of their school career. They do however still sometimes display house colours in their breast pocket handkerchiefs, when they go out to dinner.

Charterhouse boys, whose caps have been phased out, still now occasionally touch an imaginary peak, so steeped are they in the school's tradition.

Eton College may bend its uniform rules, depending on which housemaster is on duty at any given time. In addition, young Etonians wear different coloured socks to represent any new club they may start up.

What is in store for young ladies and gentlemen? What training has their early school uniform experience provided for them?

Old boys of Westminster School, perhaps the poshest of the London public schools, most frequently make their careers in the City, or in the banking and legal professions, where significantly they must wear dark business suits not so different from their schoolwear.

Old Etonians too are likely to dress poshly in their working lives, although few will wear the striped trousers of their boyhood, one famous old Etonian butler being a flamboyant exception.

One thing is certain however – young ladies and gentlemen, however old they grow, will never forget the uniform of their schooldays, for better or for worse.

Chapter 11

SCAPEGOATS OF UNIFORM

It is a fact which educationalists have sometimes overlooked that teachers in schools wear a uniform of sorts just like their pupils.

Few teachers have much dress sense, doubtless in reflection of their limited knowledge of the world. Doubtless Dr Johnson was directing at least part of his thoughts to their chalky ill-fitting gowns and slack tweeds when he described schoolmasters as: 'Children among men, men among children.' Even the distinguished poet Headmaster William Barnes (1800s) walked around with a bag over his shoulder, and a stout staff which he would shake at his pupils in class.

There have of course been teachers who have dressed in a more flamboyant style. Foremost perhaps in this category was the Head Master of Eton College (1809-1834), the infamous Dr Keate who was always birching boys on their bare bottoms, for which reason they loved to hate him, and took what vengeance they could. His costume was in fact an easy target of attack. He would regularly wear an outfit that appeared a cross between the dress of Napoleon and that of a widow woman. It was his three cornered hat and silk breeches that were most readily assaulted. When he sat down, his clothes would sometimes stick fast to a bench surface which had been smeared with cobbler's wax to this end.

Still more effective a means of ridiculing Dr Keate's dress was to emulate it. The plaster of Paris reproductions of Dr Keate in full costume peddled by street traders enraged him, but not to so great an extent as this trickster within Eton College itself:

> At dead of night, a form in cassock clad
> With gown and bands; and oh most strange of all
> In that cocked hat which marked the reverent head
> Of our Magister Informator, stood
> Before the house where that kind despot dwelt
> The very image of the owner safe in bed.

Some years later the trickster's identity was revealed as that of the Marquess of Douro, the Duke of Wellington's elder son, and so naturally a man of more blue-blooded pedigree than Dr Keate himself.

Almost as eccentrically dressed as Dr Keate was Dr A.G. Watson, the assistant master at Harrow School (1870s), who strikingly resembled the Duke of Wellington in his double-breasted frock coat, and his trousers strapped down in the old fashioned way, which he used for riding instead of riding breeches. It was perhaps for his wearing of the silk

School janitors at Merchiston Castle School, Edinburgh, 1890.

A spy cartoon of Fred W. Walker, High Master of St. Paul's, 1877-1905, who was renowned for his unsavoury habits.

Mr McDonald, the teacher of sparring, at Merchiston Castle School, 1880.

gown his Doctor of Laws degree entitled him to that he was nicknamed 'Vanity' – certainly it was for this characteristic, and not for ducal brilliance, that he was remembered.

More alarming was the Harrovian house master of the same period who would patrol the dormitories in hobnailed boots, in loud contrast to the nun whom Antonia White would recall sneaking up on pupils at Lippington, wearing 'noiseless list slippers' for the purpose.

Schoolmasters only rarely dress in ways so striking as the above, and indeed tend towards scruffiness. Head teachers naturally have the most power over what they wear personally, but few would abuse this to the extent of Mr Walker, the disgusting High Master of St Paul's Boys' School in the nineteenth century, of whom Compton Mackenzie writes: 'His clothes were stained with soup, and rank with tobacco smoke.'

Ironically, it was at St Paul's School (1890s) that one master demanded ridiculously high standards of cleanliness in the boys and once stopped a pupil formerly of his class in the corridor to whisper in his ear: 'Marcy, I am so unhappy. My form is no longer what it was. Nobody washes now. Can't you arrange to come back to me?'

More commonly masters would demand of the boys in their charge not so much supercleanliness but formal outmoded dress, as did the housemaster at Harrow who insisted his boys wore top hats and tails every week after this custom had been abolished in the rest of the school.

There was at least no hypocrisy here, as he and other masters wore outmoded dress by preference themselves. Not untypical of the period was Charles Jelf, the Headmaster of King's College School (1900s) who despised modern dress, and wore button boots, starched collars and shirts, and high choker collars. In keeping with the traditional outlook this evidenced, he was also a severe beater.

No less formidably traditional in his dress was Rutherford, Head Master of Westminster School until 1901, who has been described 'In his rustling silk gown like Olympian Zeus'.

The ordinary teacher, less powerful than the Headteacher, naturally had to succumb to the standards of dress his superior demanded of him. These have been known to be restrictive. Thus Miss Chadwick, headmistress of Oxford Central Girls' School (1900s), notoriously permitted her teaching staff neither long sleeves nor freedom from stockings, so treating them like mere pupils.

Other headmistresses will exercise their powers by personally dressing to intimidate. A former pupil of Roedean School (1920s) recalls here her old headmistress, Dame Emmeline:

> She was the traditional great Headmistress with a Queen Mary figure. She wore pince-nez and was always in gown and mortarboard. She swept majestically along the corridors like a schooner with black sails.

Not all teachers could endorse such dress, and rebel teachers will find a way, even in schools where the strictest requirements for staff's dress prevail. One lay dancing mistress at the Convent of Jesus and Mary High School, Felixstowe (1930s) defiantly wore a backless dress during lessons, and her pupils started trying to emulate her, until the Reverend

HRH The Princess Alice with the Rev. R.D. Beloe, Headmaster, Bradfield College attending the school's Sports Day, 1918.

Mother screamed blue murder, and the trendy dancing mistress was removed from her post.

Necessarily more stereotyped is the traditional school matron whom John Osborne remembers from his own schooldays as 'crisp and crackling in her white overall', and her minor idiosyncracies can make a vivid impression on children in the matron's charge. In Ian Hay's novel *The Housemaster* (1936), all matrons become one sinister creature the boys call 'The Hag', and lingering in the memory of many a former prep school pupil is the matron with stiletto heels who would be heard half way down the corridor.

Just as the matron becomes defrocked without her white starched overall, so the pedagogic monk becomes defrocked without his gown.

The gown, according to one authority, derives from the earliest monastic habit, which was Benedictine. However, the early Puritans thought differently, cursing the surplice and hood for their affinity with the dress worn by Pagan priests of Isis.

Certainly in practical terms the gown's huge hanging sleeve originally represented a civilian's growing importance in the State, while the hood was contemporaneously used to collect alms.

No less various than the theories as to the gown's origins are the theories as to its correct usage. Jesuits of Stoneyhurst, for example, have freely tucked chalk in its folds, while other religious orders would shun such a practice.

Some of the monks at Downside have been known to keep their gowns in a revolting state. Dom John, in the early part of this century, would silver the folds of his own gown with fine steel, a residue of the instruments that he crammed into his pockets.

As in the case of many monks, Dom John's attachment to his gown went beyond the bounds of reason. He demonstrated this characteristically when after returning to Downside from serving in World War II. He could not find his gown on his normal peg. He picked up the gown on a nearby peg instead, and moths flew out of its folds into the semi-darkness, causing Dom John to grumble: 'If only people wouldn't move things about when one goes away.' The garment was, however, not his.

Just as the monk has his gown, so the nun has her habit. This can prove cumbersome, as when a girl during a swimming lessons at Holy Child Convent, St. Leonard-on-Sea (1940s) appeared to be drowning, so the supervising nun promptly bellyflopped fully habited into the water to save her.

Her habit billowed in the waters like the sails of a capsized yacht, and the pupils watching her rescue attempt clapped and cheered mightily. Lo and behold, the apparent drowning victim was laughing with the rest.

There are, however, schoolteachers who attract contempt from their pupils on a more regular basis. Mr McEachran, the English master at Shrewsbury School (1940s) notoriously dressed like a tramp, which he passed off as poetic licence claiming personal acquaintance with the

Mr Holloway, the village blacksmith, with pupils of Bradfield College, gathered round the anvil watching a snake being forged in a 1920s design and technology class.

contemporary poet W.H. Auden, who opined that teachers should give up wearing 'ridiculous black clothes... which make them look like unsuccessful insurance agents.'

Nonetheless, Mr McEachran cut a distinctively unimpressive figure in class and would have done well to take a leaf out of the book of tidier teachers, such as his contemporary at Bristol Grammar School, the white haired head of Classics, the Reverend Collins, who wore his gown and mortar board to every lesson long after this was normal practice, for which he was nicknamed 'the Saint'.

Another saintly dresser was one woodwork teacher described here by an eye witness:

> His suit was immaculate, his shirt and tie impeccable, his cuffs protruded exactly the right amount, his socks were discreet, and his shoes shone like mirrors. You will not be surprised to learn that he was a late entrant to the profession, having spent many years in the City.

This was to dress better than can be expected of the most conscientious teachers, who are not, after all, paid to be fashion models. Doubtless the schoolmaster who manicured his toenails and polished his sandals in class was going too far, and actually setting his pupils a bad example.

There comes a stage whereat pupils will quite openly persecute their masters who don't dress the part. A Winchester Latin master turned up to class once without his gown, which left him open to having a Latin dictionary thrown at him. A pupil, who happened to be Tim Brooke-Taylor, later of *the Goodies*, obliged by hitting him slap on the face with a volume that turned out to be the Latin master's own.

Pupils at Downside mocked Osmond Egmode, the master who walked around with an emerald ring on his finger and a crimson skull cap on his head, for which combination he was nicknamed 'the Cardinal'. His Downside contemporary, Dom Watson Richards, was designated 'a pigeon' in his black woollen wraps and knitted skull cap. Certainly the lot of the eccentrically dressed schoolteacher was not always a happy one.

So set in their ways were some schoolmasters that they always dressed in their schoolmasterly garb, even on occasions of leisure. In this respect the Winchester schoolmaster Dean Runnell went too far, and when he was about to change into evening dress for a party, he would have second thoughts about going, and would get into his bed without changing.

If the average schoolteacher could hide behind his garb and command respect, the average school porter could not. Soon after his arrival at Bristol Grammar School as headmaster, Doctor Norwood decided that the head porter, known as 'school sergeant', should wear uniform. The next day, the sergeant brought a boy up before the headmaster to be punished for insolence. Upon inquiry, it appeared that as the sergeant was passing, the boy had put his head out from behind a pillar and had called out 'Buttons'.

Boys have not dared to be so cheeky to their teachers, unless they should run across them again by chance in their adult years. On one recent such occasion, an Ampleforth monk met one of his old boys at a wedding and said cattily: 'You were always one of the dim ones.'

The old boy, a successful self-employed decorator, retorted: 'You can't talk, hiding behind your cowl.' This barb hit home, and the holy man turned beetroot.

An adult perspective on schoolmasters' dressing habits reveals them for what they are, backward and unworldly for the most part. Some may pity the schoolmasters at Uppingham for instance who take pride in the battered states of their gowns, and we are reminded here of the schoolmaster Mr Chips, sentimentally described in this extract from James Hilton's famous novel *Goodbye Mr Chips*:

> He wore his gown 'till it was almost too tattered to hold together; and when he stood on the wooden bench by big hall steps to take call over, it was with an air of a mystic abandonment to ritual.

Nonetheless as parents, we like to see our children's masters wear gowns to represent the acquisition of a university degree, which is still valued in educational circles. Quite understandably, Stanley Gregory, Headmaster of Chatham Grammar School for Boys, urges his staff, when so entitled, to wear gowns at prizegiving ceremonies, because this little touch impresses parents.

Teachers themselves will sometimes envy each other's dress, leading to blossoming conflicts in the isolated hothouse communities of schools throughout the country.

One schoolmaster's resentment of another's dress may indeed symbolise resentment of youth, of popularity, or of a dozen other attributes.

The sheer intensity of it all is well represented in this extract from Hugh Walpole's masterly novel *Mr Perrin and Mr Traill*, wherein the elderly schoolmaster regards his younger professional colleague:

> Then suddenly his eye fell on Traill, and that moment must be recorded as the first instant of his dislike. Traill was absurd, quite absurd – over-dressed, in fact.
>
> His hair was brushed and parted so that you could almost see your face in brown glossiness. His coat fitted amazingly. There was a wonderful white waistcoat with pearl buttons, there were wonderful silk socks with pale blue clocks, there was a splendid even line of white cuff below the sleeves.
>
> But Perrin was forced to admit that this smartness was not common; it was quite natural, as though Traill had always worn clothes like that. Could it be that Perrin was shabby... not that Traill was smart?
>
> Perrin dragged his cuffs from their dark hiding places, then saw there was a new frayed piece that had escaped his scissors, and pushed them back again.

As, nowadays, schools become supposedly more in touch with industry and with the outside world, so should teachers' dress. Wearing shabby clothes due to chalk dust in the classroom is no longer the excuse that it was since chalk is being replaced by fibretip marker pens. Academic licence is no excuse either since university academics, the real intellectuals, dress quite nattily. It is significant that unsuitably dressed staff at St. Mary's Comprehensive School, Menston, where the author taught as a student, are sent home, just like unsuitably dressed pupils.

While a minority of teachers is well dressed nowadays, like the masters of Eton College in their dark grey suits and gowns with wing collars and white bow ties, others remain archaically and shabbily dressed, and it is often these who are sticklers for the correct uniform to be worn by the pupils, forbidding them to undo top buttons or to remove blazers in class. What is not generally known is that enforcement of uniform regulations in state schools has no legal basis, but tough, ill-dressed schoolmasters nonetheless often successfully carry it out.

Similarly, it is often the shabbiest looking matrons who carry out nit-checks on pupils the most vigorously, and it may only be the attractively dressed matrons who will generously wash boys' clothes until they fade to a fashionable hue, as they do with boys' corduroy jackets at the Dragon School.

There is a contemporary ring of truth in this pearl of wisdom from the lips of William Lamb, second Viscount Melbourne: 'It is tiresome to hear education discussed, tiresome to educate, and tiresome to be educated.' Perhaps this is why teachers still often take so little trouble to dress decently.

Chapter 12

A WELL WORN THEME IN LITERATURE

School uniform is to be found everywhere, and not least in books. The acclaimed Victorian poet Swinburne was in adult life obsessed with the floggings he had witnessed or undergone at Eton, and in his less acclaimed verses he has celebrated these, drooling over removal of school uniform in all its thrilling detail. Here is an extract from his notorious 'Flogging by Etoniensis':

> Seventeen years of age, with round limbs, and
> broad, tall, rosy and fair,
> And all over his forehead and temples,
> A forest of curly red hair,
> Good in the playing fields, good on the
> water, or in it, lad.
> But at sums or at themes, or at verses, oh ain't
> Charlie Collingwood bad!
> Six days out of seven or five at the least, he's sent
> up to be stripped;
> But it's nuts for the lower boys always to see
> Charlie Collingwood whipped;
> For the marks of the birch on his bottom are
> more than the leaves on a tree,
> And a bum that has worn so much birch
> out as Charlie's is jolly to see.
> When his shirt is turned up and his breeches,
> unbuttoned hang down to his heels,
> From the small of his back to the thick of his
> thighs is one mass of red weals.
> Ted Beauchamp, last year, began keeping
> a list of his floggings and he says they came
> in a year-and-a-half to a hundred and sixty three.
> And you see how this morning in front of the flogging
> block silent he stands,
> And hitches his waistband up slightly,
> and feels his backside with his hands.

The gradual removal of school uniform to bare Charlie Collingwood's bottom for his next flogging, is suffused here with erotic implication.

There are other, less orthodox rituals involving removal of school uniform, that are heavy with sexual innuendo. John Osborne recalls in this extract from his autobiography, *A Better Class of Person*, the *modus operandi* of one child virago and her gang at Elmsleigh Road School:

> The victim, almost always a boy, was dragged to a suitably public place like
> the middle of the playground or playing field, and, spread-eagled, he would
> have to endure the humiliation of Daphne lifting up her skirt and placing her

navy blue gusset firmly on his head. She would sit like a conquering hunter for as long as it suited her with the cold frenzy of a goddess on heat for sacrifice while her prey gave up the struggle against asphyxiation. She might even urge her slaves to remove the victim's shorts.

Still more rumbustious are the infamous St. Trinian girls, dressed in gymslips, who brandish their lacrosse nets at all and sundry. As one of their official rhymsters Sidney Gilliat puts it:

Maidens of St. Trinians
Gird your armour on
Grab the nearest weapon
Never mind which one!
The battle's to the strongest
Might is always right
Trample on the weakest
Glory in their plight!
St. Trinians! St. Trinians!
Our battle cry.
St. Trinians! St. Trinians!
Will never die!

Here of course is an example of the famous gymslips being evoked without even a mention of them, but school uniform may of course be referred to more directly. Alec Waugh analyses the role of school uniform in the public schools in his famous first novel *The Loom of Youth*, which he wrote when he was only seventeen years old and had just left Sherborne.

In the novel, school uniform, with its variations in style and colour to represent stages of the hierarchy within the school, appears sacred, and the 'Chief' (i.e. Headmaster) furiously descends on any boy who wears another's clothes.

Nor is assault on another's dress acceptable, as Lovelace here makes clear in this denunciation of the junior who has knocked off Gordon's hat:

The little swine! He is not fit to be in a decent school. If he can't get rid of the habits he learnt with street cads in the holidays of his own accord, he'll have to be kicked out of them. We will wait for him one day, and if we see him knock a School House straw off, my God, we will boot him to blazes!

The school uniform regulations are more relaxed at the imaginary Greyfriars School, where Billy Bunter and his cronies have had most of their adventures over a span of thirty years.

Billy Bunter, as becomes clear from texts and the illustrations alike, not only wears the tightest trousers at Greyfriars School and in the county of Kent, but his alone are crossed horizontally and vertically. Generally his dress is erratic to reflect his character.

In fact schoolchildren in literature are often characterised by their dress. It is in keeping with Evelyn Waugh's satirical intent that in his early masterpiece *Decline and Fall*, the pupils of Llanedba Preparatory School are described as wearing Eton suits and dinner jackets in evidence of their breeding.

Just as prestigious is the school blazer, as evoked in this scene from Simon Raven's novel *Fielding Gray*, after the public schoolboy Grey has just joined his parents on the cricket field where he has been playing against Eton:

"Feeling ill?" asked Wharton. "Oh, no!" answered Bunter. "I—I'd like another cigar, but—but perhaps it would spoil my lunch. I—I think I'll go to my room. I—I feel a little giddy!"

Frank Richards' famous character Billy Bunter indisposed after indulging in an illicit cigar. This 1930 cartoon appeared in The Magnet.

Somerset Maugham aged fifteen, at The King's School, Canterbury.

'All that blue,' said my father, eying my blazer and costing it to the nearest sixpence. 'Anyone would think you were playing for the Varsity at Lord's.'
'And so he might,' my mother said, 'If he goes on like this.'

Of course schoolwear in literature can be put to more practical purpose. In James Joyce's famous novel *Portrait of the Artist as a Young Man*, when Stephen Dedalus complains of an unfair beating, the official acknowledgement that he is right seems miraculous, and all the schoolboys celebrate by flinging their caps high into the air.

More resourceful than these schoolboys is the audacious Julie, described in this extract from Ian McKewan's acclaimed first novel, *The Cement Garden*:

> In the evenings she often stayed at home to wash her hair and iron the pleats in her navy blue school skirt. She was one of a handful of daring girls at school who wore starched white petticoats beneath their skirts to fill them out and make them swirl when they turned on their heel. She wore stockings and black knickers, strictly forbidden.

While Julie turned school uniform to her advantage, other characters in literature have found cause to curse it. In one memorable scene from Barry Hines' novel *Kes*, the comprehensive school Headmaster frisks boys for cigarettes, in what seems almost a tampering with their schoolwear. Longer suffering, however, is the eponymous heroine of Stephen King's famous first novel *Carrie*.

Carrie is teased to distraction, and her school uniform becomes first to show the strain. Her underpants are hidden from her reach, and snakes

Cricket team, Portora Royal School, 1923. Samuel Beckett seated right.

curl up in her shoes. When she kneels to pray, the zipper of her skirt splits, making an exaggerated sound of breaking wind.

Carrie suffers her most terrifying humiliation, the pig's blood bath, when she is fabulously dressed for the school dance. We can only stand by in sympathy as she wreaks her telekinetic vengeance.

The rejection of standard school uniform is a popular theme in school literature, and is accurately represented as a cause of controversy. In Sue Townsend's bestselling book *The Secret Diary of Adrian Mole*, the teenage protagonist and his friends turn up at school one day wearing illicit red communist socks, much to the Headmaster's horror:

> Pop eyed Scouten must have been tipped off because he was waiting in the fourth year cloakroom. He was standing very still with his arms folded, staring with poached egg eyes. He didn't speak, he just nodded upstairs. All the red socks trooped upstairs.

Even when a child is permitted deviation from the school uniform norm by the teachers, he or she may stick out like a sore thumb amongst peers. In Muriel Spark's famous novel *The Prime of Miss Jean Brodie*, a new pupil who has a record of being expelled from many schools, wears dark green clothes, instead of the usual violet uniform:

> Joyce Emily's parents, wealthy as they were, had begged for a trial period to elapse before investing in yet another set of school uniform clothing for their daughter.

Is doing without uniform the answer? In Miles Franklin's novel *My Brilliant Career*, children attending the Australian Bush School would

A humorous pose struck by scholars of Bishop's Stortford School, 1896.

walk around barefoot, and this authentic stigma roused deep resentment in the protagonist.

Rejection of school uniform is clearly more satisfying for those who have been swamped with it. In Rebecca Irvine's *The Girl's Guide to the English Public Schoolboy*, the token toff Jenkins has always dressed correctly at his public school, but upon leaving it he betrays the ideal:

> by flinging together a riotous assembly of hues which have been at loggerheads since time began. Even the knickers may be day-glo, or worse, have Union Jacks on them.

However literature, like the real live situations that give rise to it, will never entirely escape from the formative influence of school uniform, and the author feels privileged to make here his own humble contribution in the form of this book.

Chapter 13

THE LANGUAGE OF SCHOOLS

An heraldic device conveys a school's image to the outside world, and its symbolism, apparently obscure, may often be gleaned from age-old traditions.

It is indeed for the prestige of its origin that this device is so treasured within school, becoming embossed not just on the school blazer, but also on the backs of chairs, on honours boards, and in other important places.

It is not generally known in these schools that the right to bear an heraldic device must be granted by the King of Arms. According to an investigative report in 1983, thirty-seven major public schools, including St. Paul's, Winchester, Charterhouse and Marlborough had not obtained this permission. It has however been clarified that a school may display the arms of founders and benefactors, provided that it does not claim these are the arms of the school.

School arms are most commonly suffused with religious symbolism. The heraldic device of St Lawrence's College is typically pious, showing a celestial crown representing the crown of life, an open book representing the Bible, and a shell as the pilgrim's emblem, together with two crosses, fundamental insignia of Christianity.

Prominent amongst further religious symbolism are the serpent and the dove on the Radley College arms, the crossed keys, emblem of St. Peter on the Ampleforth arms, and the black cross on the arms of the King's School Canterbury, together with the letters I and X to recall that the Cathedral is dedicated to Jesus Christ. The cross and the book on the arms of St Margaret's School, Bushey, are emblems of the saintly Queen Margaret, after whom the school was named.

The lamb representing John the Baptist and two camels as a source of hair for his clothes are presented in combination of the arms of the Merchant Taylors' School, together with the lion of England.

Animal symbolism is found further on many coats of arms, and the commonest bird portrayed is the eagle. The raven with a ring in his beak on the arms of Ellesmere College is the messenger sent by the saintly King Oswald to a heathen princess he wished to convert and marry.

The pigeons on the arms of Dean Close School represent a more prosaic legend, namely the discovery of the mineral waters to which Cheltenham owed its rise as an inland watering place.

Amongst more earthbound creatures represented on school crests are the black greyhounds on the arms of Solihull School, the scarlet wolves on those of Hurstpierpoint College, and the muzzled grey bear standing on his hind legs on the crest of Warwick School.

The arms of Radley College, Oxon.

Unique is the lizard on the crest of Skinner's School. Due to its spots, the creature has been wrongly represented as a leopard, with widespread consequences. Pupils have called themselves 'leopards', the school magazine is *The Leopard*, and the Old Boys' Club is the 'Guild of Leopards'.

Although misinterpretation in this case is deliberate, in other cases it may not be. Sources of arms are frequently uncertain. For instance, the yellow birds on the Repton College crest have been presumed eagles, pigeons or birds of unknown genus respectively. Uncertainty of interpretation can lead to a change in coats of arms, such as Merchant Taylors' School opted for, on grounds that its original crest was 'overmuch intricate with confused mixtures of too many things in one shield, contrary to the loved and commendable manner of bearing arms.' Such a drastic step was however not so common as re-interpretation.

Reinterpretation may not always enhance the prestige of the arms under scrutiny. The arms of St. Paul's Boys' School became subject to a former pupil's reinterpretation in *The Pauline* of December 1882, on the grounds that the chevron was not engrailed (i.e. indented), but plain, making for a much more common heraldic bearing.

In fact, if the truth be known, many a respected school has arms that portray a lowly origin, and in particular the Cathedral schools, of which only Westminster feels no need to display the Cathedral's arms on its pupils' blazers.

Outside the Cathedral schools, particularly prominent is the bunch of dates in a lion's paw on the crest of Rugby School, designating the trade of grocer by which the school's founder had made his fortune, and for which Queen Elizabeth I had mercilessly teased him.

Likewise, the crest of Colfe's School betrays a common origin, insofar as it is traceable to the ancient Colfe's family. However, a second coat of arms, that of the original leatherseller, is available to the school as well.

More obscurely but as unequivocally, the arms of Mill Hill School show humble roots, by depicting martlets without feet to indicate that the school had no endowment but the land on which its building stood. Their purpose is here described by Guillem, an early writer on heraldry:

> To put them (the pupils) in mind to trust their wings of vertue and merit, to raise themselves and not their legges, having little land to put their feet on.

Of course, the crest can offer symbolic rescue from poverty. There are purses on the arms of Lancing College, which represent those given by St. Nicholas as dowries to three daughters of an impoverished nobleman, to save them from poverty and from shame.

Particularly dignified are the crests of schools founded to educate the poor. The arms of Emanuel School, which falls into this category, represent the arms of thirteen knights, each of whom has played his part in English history and is connected with the rest by overlap of family trees.

Education generally is well represented in the symbolism of school arms. The open book on the crest of Epsom College signifies learning. The open book, the seven branched candlestick, and the tablets of stone all on Carmel College's crest stand for learning, enlightenment, and observance respectively. The lilies on Eton College's crest are flowers of every kind of knowledge, belonging also to the Virgin Mary, to whom the school was dedicated.

Knowledge is not always the priority in public schools, particularly where the education has a tradition of liaison with the Services. Gordonstoun's crest shows a bireme, the ship of war in Ancient Greece, which is true to form since Gordonstoun boys have traditionally practised seamanship as an activity sometimes leading to a profession, and it was the Greek way of life that had influenced the Headmaster Dr. Hahn in becoming a schoolmaster in his middle age.

Another ancient ship of war, in this case black with red pennons and flags, appears on the arms of the Davenport Foundation School. In a similar tradition, the crest of Oswestry School represents a grey shield, as used in battle.

A bloodthirsty source of arms need not necessarily involve war, as is manifest in the implication of the hand on the badge of Ulster which is shown on the arms of Sir Walter St. John's School, and Battersea Grammar School. This hand commemorates the legend wherein it was decreed that the first of two Viking chiefs to touch the soil of Ireland would be lord of the land. At the point where there were only yards to go in the race for possession, and the ships were still level, one of the rivals cut off his own left hand with his sword, and threw it ashore. For this, he became Lord of Ireland, and his hand became the badge of the province of Ulster.

Usually printed under the school crest is the school motto, whose source may well be frivolous. Repton College's motto, *Porta vicat culpa* derives from a ridiculous pun on a line of Ovid made by the school's first Headmaster, the learned and pedantic Reverend Joseph Gould, during a Latin lesson.

The meanings of mottos may be ambiguous. Shrewsbury's school motto, reading *Latus si recte,* is construable by the loyal as: 'If your conscience is all right, don't work', but by the lazy as: 'If you're all right don't work'.

Indeed mottos may be duplicated. The motto usually attributed to Eton College is *Floreat Etona,* meaning 'May Eton prosper', but many prefer the alternative *Esto perpetua,* i.e. 'Last thou forever'.

The motto's most commonplace theme is religion, and a motto of this kind may exhort pupils of the school. For instance, Charterhouse's motto *Deo dante dedi,* meaning 'God giving, I have given', reflects the founder's wish to get into heaven as a result of his own giving, with an implication that the boys must give in return for God's gift of Charterhouse.

Religious mottos are sometimes rammed down pupils' throats. At one convent the pupils had to write the school motto *Ad Maiorem Dei Gloriam,* meaning 'To the Greater Glory of God', on the top of every written exercise the nuns set them. Most didn't even know what it meant.

'Action not words' was the motto of Holy Child Convent, St. Leonards-on-Sea (1940s), which provoked one pupil to comment: 'Once I'm out of here, I'll hang that motto over my bed'.

Mottos in the strict Catholic schools are where possible perverted by the children, like the proud motto of St. Benedict's Ealing, *Laborare est Orare,* meaning 'To work is to pray', which has been translated as 'Lavatory and orifice'.

SOME SCHOOL MOTTOS

Striving Towards Achievement:
Gordonstoun School: *Plus est en Vous* (There is more in you)
King's School, Canterbury: *Age dum Agis* (Work while you are about it)
Mill Hill School: *Et Virtutem et Musas* (Character and Culture)
Shrewsbury School: *Latus si recte ne labora* (If your conscience is right, don't worry)
Solihull School: *Perseverantia* (Perseverance)
Warwick School: *Alteriora Peto* (I aim at Higher Things)

Striving for God's Approval:
Ampleforth College: *Dieu le Ward* (This motto is not generally used today, and is a pun on Dieulouard, the continental home of the forerunner of Ampleforth Abbey)
Bruton School for Girls (Sunny Hill School): Follow the Gleam
Clifton College: *Spiritus Intus Alit* (The Spirit Nourisheth Within)

Colfe's Grammar School: *Soli Deo Honor et Gloria* (Honour and Glory for God Alone)

Dean Close School: *Verbum Dei Lucerna* (The Word of God is a Lantern)

Epsom College: *Deo Non Fortuna* (Not through Luck but through the Help of God)

Haileybury & Imperial Service College: *Sursum Corda* (Lift up your Hearts)

Hurstpierpoint College: *Beati Mundo Corde* (Blessed are the Poor in Heart)

Merchant Taylors' School: *Homo Plantat, Homo Irrigat, sed Deus dat Incrementum* (Man Planteth and Watereth, but God giveth Increase)

St. Margaret's School, Bushey: *Sursum Corda: Habemus ad Dominum* (Lift up your Hearts: We have Lifted them up to the Lord)

Sir Thomas Rich's School, Gloucester: *Garde Ta Foy* (Keep Faith)

Sir Walter St. John's School, Battersea: Rather Deathe than False of Faythe

Skinners' School: To God Only be all Glory

Work and Religious ethic combined:
Rugby School: *Orando Laborando* (By Prayer and Work)
St. Benedict's, Ealing: *Laborare est Orare* (To Work is to Pray)
St. Paul's Boys' School: *Fide et Literis* (by faith and by letters)

Patriotism, Gentlemanliness and Innocence:
Archbishop Holgate's Grammar School, York: *Vincet Amor Patriae* (Love of One's Country Conquers)

Brentwood School: Virtue, Learning, Manners

Ellesmere College: *Pro Patria Dimicans* (Striving for one's Country)

Oxford Central Girls' School & Cheney Girls' Grammar School: *Vitam Impendere Vero* (Devote your Life to Truth)

Rodbourne College: *Gratia Plena* (Full of Force)

Summer Fields: *Mens Sana in Corpore Sano* (A Healthy Mind in a Healthy Body)

Woodbridge School: *Pro Deo Rege Patria* (For God, King and Country)

Self-Congratulating:
Eton College: *Floreat Etona* (May Eton Prosper)
Oratory School: *Cor ad Cor Loquitur* (The Heart speaks to the Heart)
Oswestry School: D. Holbache: *Ffundatore: MCCCCVII* (Holbache, Founder, 1407)

Less formal than the school mottos, but of infinitely greater practical use in the language of school uniform is school slang, which helps to keep the school self-sufficient.

Such slang finds its most fertile breeding ground in the top public boarding-schools, which have been traditionally most isolated from the world in any case. The Harrovian still adds 'er' on to words designating specified garments, so grey trousers become 'greysers' and blue flannel coats 'bluers'. Furthermore at Harrow School, top hats are toppers, silk facings are 'silkers', and waistcoats are 'wekkers'. Such a wide ranging slang has been matched by other public schools, including Winchester in the 1930s, where top hats became 'cathedrals' or 'cathers', bowler hats were 'cowshooters', and the brown bowlers of an earlier era were still referred to as 'good godsters'.

In many schools, informal wear has had its slang epithets. At Westminster School it is known as 'shag'; at The Royal Russell School Purley, it is 'scruff rig'; Etonians wear 'standard change', and Sherborne's boys 'mufti'.

Far more subtle than school slang is the language of colours, which in relation to school uniform is as yet relatively unresearched. However, certainly governors and Headmasters of schools prefer the uniform to be of conservative hue, often black and grey – the traditional colours of clergymen's and solicitor's dress, which have the additional advantage of not showing dirt too easily.

School blazers are frequently blue, as are sometimes school shirts, coats and ties. This is a calm and respectable colour, conveying the sobriety of the Conservative Party whose official colour is blue and the gentleness of the Virgin Mary, characteristically portrayed in religious art as dressed in this colour.

Many school uniforms such as that of Gad's Hill School, have items of brown which represent affinity with the earth, thus helping to foster stability.

Girls at Red Maids' School, Bristol, wearing their red cloaks and bonnets.

Rare but striking is red in school uniform, still to be found in the cloaks worn by the girls of the Red Maids' School in Bristol, surviving unchanged since the sixteenth century.

Less striking but nonetheless unmistakeable is the claret in the colours of Wellingborough School, Northants, which has led to the school's being renamed 'The Plum School'.

Red actually causes a rise of blood pressure in anyone who looks at it, and Goethe, in his theory of colours, has commented: 'Amongst savage nations, the inclination for it has been universally marked'.

Schoolchildren in our Western civilisation, not being savages, are protected by what they must wear. Indeed one function of dress, according to the costume psychologist Flugel, is to protect the wearer from moral danger. This may apply to Flugel's monk in his habit, but it must be remembered that the child in school uniform has not chosen similarly to renounce the world. The decision has been made for him.

Chapter 14

UNIFORM ON THE MOVE

Over the ages there has been no more colourful sight in schools than gameswear, which in bygone days was less standardised and more flamboyant, reflecting the laxer regulations by which school games were then played.

At one stage, children would dress for school specifically in preparation for sports. Here is an authentic description of a fifteenth century schoolboy being dressed in the morning for school:

> Eman: Give me the single thickness so that I may be less heavy for playing ball (pila) today.
>
> Beat: This is always your custom. You think of your play before your schoolwork.
>
> Eman: What do you say, you stupid! When school itself is called play (ludus).

Sadly for the children, most ordinary schoolwear was not designed for rough sports and would be scathed by it, perhaps even irretrievably.

In particular the cumbersome soutanes, compulsorily worn tucked in at the waist by pupils of seventeenth century St. Omers, now Stonyhurst, were not able to withstand being roughed around. Despite this, pupils played football in these soutanes, cheerfully dribbling, tackling and shooting in a lofty disregard for their sanctified cloth. Naturally, the soutanes flapped free of the boys' waists, their tail ends becoming ragged and muddy. Most shockingly of all, the school corridors became littered with bits of these gowns.

The school authorities swiftly forbade this practice, and, perhaps to inflict a penance, inaugurated an amazing custom on the cricket field. When the angelus sounded during a game, the boys had instantly to freeze their play, and smartly to raise their caps. As was intended, prospective parents were impressed.

It seems that the school learned from its mistakes, and pupils of Stoneyhurst in the nineteenth century were allowed to wear old clothes for the murky sport of 'pogging' which was a form of fishing actually involving participants wading through the water. Old cricket suits were most popularly used, and so it was no great loss when they were irreparably damaged from waterlogging.

Wearing old clothes, not specifically school gameswear, for sports sanctioned by a school can cause offence. Etonians for instance used to go hunting clad in rustic tweed jackets and breeches, which led to outraged complaints from local farmers who were dressed in exactly the same way.

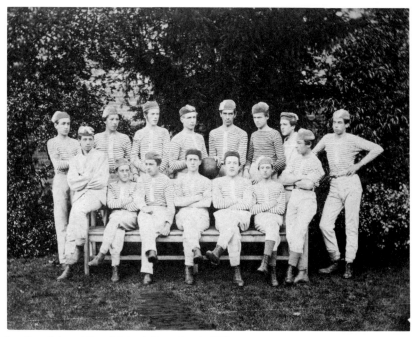

Sporting stripes at Forest School, Snaresbrook, 1867.

Wearing no clothes at all can understandably be still more offensive to the public, although Etonians right up to 1936 would be encouraged to swim naked in public places. In the Victorian era, one Etonian schoolboy, George Eden Hunt, swam naked towards the island called Ditton Park in search of ducks' eggs, but was spotted by an irate farmer, and, not having time to retrieve his clothes, raced back to Eton College's premises stark naked.

Of course, colourful informal dress for school sports can charm the public, provided it poses no threat to it, and none fitted this bill better than Harrow's green costume used for archery sessions, with its suggestion of hunters' camouflaging dress for the forest, as Robin Hood wore.

Still more colourful and just as famous throughout England was the bright fancy dress, which frequently took the form of a clown's costume, worn by the horseracers in Shrewsbury School's steeplechase.

Despite a later decree carried to ban such 'colours', the huntsman of the runs continued to wear cap, sweater, and stockings of the traditional runs. Whilst he and his whips carried horns and hunting crops, the 'gentlemen' bore their batons, and, most endearingly of all, ordinary clothes were transported in a donkey cart, as described here by a former participant:

> A grey form was observed slowly making its way forward, which from the serpentine method of progress was immediately recognised as the donkey; relieved thus from anxiety, we began to strip.

The Cricket XI of Bradfield College, Reading 1858.

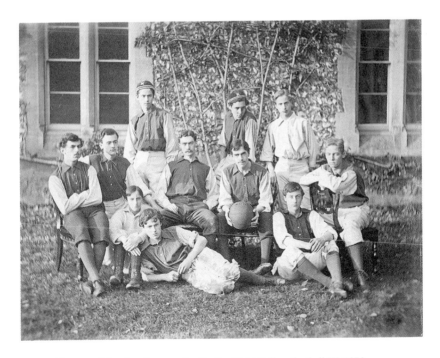

A relaxed pose straight after the game for the Bradfield College football XI, 1878.

Schoolchildren of this period played many games without dressing specially for them, but it is necessarily in the clothes designed for standard school sports that the weird and wonderful prototypes of the species are found. In *The Decline of the Aristocracy*, Arthur Ponsonby offers us this following observation:

> If it is a football eleven they will be in varied and strange garments, with their trousers tucked into their socks, some with ill-fitting caps and old shrunken shirts, others perhaps neater, but each one individual and distinct.

Such clothes sometimes had an unsavoury purpose. The garish stripes of the Forest School football team's shirt were designed to frighten the opposition, as were the hooped jerseys of the football team of King's School, Rochester, although the King's School rugby team was supposed to be presenting a less aggressive image with a skull and crossbones embroidered on the shirt, intended merely as a lucky mascot.

Indeed, outlandish gameswear was the norm in schools of the Victorian era. Footballers of Winchester College wore striped shirts, while Harrovians sported white trousers and black gaiters. Eastbourne College's football team wore a jersey with dark blue and white horizontal stripes, which towards the end of the nineteenth century was replaced by a dark blue shirt, following this radical proposition raised in the school magazine of November 1884:

> Since almost every Association Club now wears the shirt, instead of the jersey, I propose that our eleven should also substitute the shirt for the jersey.

Boys of this era played football and rugby in trousers, or else, as at Clifton, with their knees covered. Perhaps uniquely, Repton footballers tucked the ends of their long flannel trousers into their socks during games, so that they looked like cyclists without clips.

Shorts were introduced to team players in the 1880s in the form of knickerbockers, and at Radley College, as elsewhere, they took some getting used to.

Primitive dress was appropriate for a primitive form of games, and Rugbeian footballers were amongst its most enthusiastic exponents, donning what was described in the school magazine of 1848 as strange velvet caps and a disordered assortment of jerseys. It did not however end here. Here is an extract from *Tom Brown's Schooldays*, describing the Rugbeians gleefully making final preparations, as if for a scuffle, although actually for a football match:

> They are hanging their jackets, and all who mean real work, their hats, waistcoats, neck handkerchiefs, and braces on the railings.

As was to be expected, the Rugbeians would play rough. They wore ironshod football boots called navvies which they put to good use, not just for running or for punting the ball, but also for hacking shins. Indeed one teamplayer, as recalled by Guillemard, played so foul that the referee threatened to substitute his navvies with carpet slippers.

Studs, officially banned until 1891, were unofficially alive and kicking decades earlier, as a former pupil of a preparatory school in Rugby elucidates in this extract from a letter he wrote at the time:

A flamboyant football twenty at Marlborough College, 1867.

Five sporting champions at Wellington College, 1899.

A rather apprehensive new boy dressed for football at Merchiston Castle School, Edinburgh, 1890.

A gymnasium group, St. Paul's School, 1892. The stripes on the boys' vests have a very modern appearance.

> I got a piece of about 3/4 of an inch long taken right out of my leg. The fellow
> who did it must have had nails in his boots which are not allowed.

Other dangers from boots were legion, and Sir A.D. Astley witnessed at
Eton College in this era a boot flying slap into the face of a player on the
opposing team.

Certainly, these games were a hit and miss affair, and were all the time
applauded by other pupils made to watch from the sidelines, supervised
by po-faced prefects who, at Rugby School for instance, would lash out
with canes at the first sign of disorder.

Boys who distinguished themselves during a match would be
awarded colours, perhaps in the form of flannels, which a wearer has
designated in this context a 'comfort in more ways than one'.

After matches and award ceremonies alike, colours would celebrate
by downing ale until they were all in their cups. This was one of many
privileges extended to colours at Rugby School and elsewhere. Colours
of Westminster School uniquely were permitted to wear headgear as and
when they wished, which was a concession indeed.

Even the weaker boys who were useless at sports were forced to play
them, with a frequency and a hardness that seems barbaric by today's
standards, at public schools such as Harrow, and to a lesser degree, Eton.
To this end, a house notice at Eton College (1870s) read:

> Any lower boy in this house who does not play football once daily, and twice a
> day on half holidays, will be fined half a crown and be kicked.

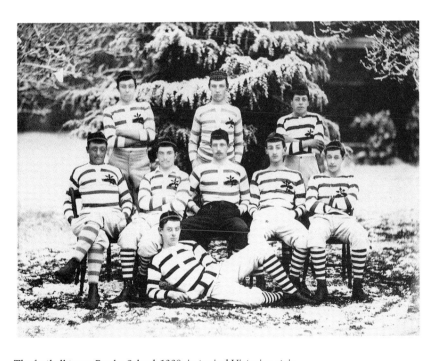

The football team, Rugby School, 1880, in typical Victorian strip.

The Paperchase Champion, Rugby School, 1886.

It is no wonder that many public school boys found relief in the summer cricket, which was sometimes more leisurely than the winter sports, and for which they were permitted to dress more charmingly, in reflection of their social origins.

Cricketers of Eton and Harrow wore snobbish straw hats, and cricketers of Winchester wore toppers. If colour schemes sometimes clashed, they were at least relatively freely chosen, and members of the Douai cricket teams for instance looked relaxed and liberated with full ties round their waists, and half ties hanging from their collars.

Even at this stage patterns had started to emerge in school cricket wear, which would solidify over the decades to come, making up the tradition of a uniform.

These traditions were pervaded with sentiment, and typically, the silver buckle of 1850s Repton headmaster Steuart Adolphus Pears was handed down to succeeding generations of cricket captains in his name.

Schoolgirls of this era and later, like their male counterparts, dressed flatteringly for cricket. They often wore pink bloomers, or knickerbockers. Here is the protagonist of *Coming Through the Rye* speaking for a generation:

> We are all upstairs... and putting on knickerbockers and blouses. Yes knickerbockers! Let no one blush or be shocked, for they are long and ample, and tied modestly in at the ankle!

For tennis, girls wore attractive aprons made with pockets to hold spare balls. In the gymnasium, they would remove long skirts and cumber-

The hockey team at The Girls' Grammar School, Bradford, 1902.

Lady cricketers resplendent in their boaters at St. Mary's Hall, Brighton, 1903.

Three sporting girls at Bedales School, Petersfield, 1906.

some clothes, and some pupils of the Royal Naval School, so divested during one gym lesson, were subsequently confronted with an official photographer, whereupon the mistress in charge darted into the corner to put on her own skirt before she would allow her picture to be taken.

Such modesty was prevalent amongst pupils as well as their mistresses in girls' schools of this era, and in the formative years of school uniforms' development, girls were prohibited from dressing to look sexy, even more than they are today. Such conservatism is demonstrated in the following extract from St. Paul's Girls' School's swimming bath regulations (1909):

> If the dress is made in two pieces, there must be provision for fastening the two together very firmly.

Boys of this period had more leeway, and an Eton dame considered that members of the College's Boating VIII looked so delicious that they had to have been selected for the team on grounds of sex appeal alone.

Male sex appeal went hand in hand with the macho image, and schoolboys of the early twentieth century were expected to endure hardship, even bullying. Typically, at Bedales, seniors would slap 'trademarks' on younger boys' bare backs, in the changing rooms.

Indeed, L.P. Hartley recalls from his schooldays at Harrow the tradition that each pupil should work himself into a muddy sweaty state during his free afternoon, pointing out:

> If a fez (i.e. a colour) saw one slink in spick-and-span and unruffled he might give one a black look or a word of caution, usually phrased in the most wounding terms; but nothing else happened.

Not surprisingly in this climate, shinpads, introduced with good reason into football uniform, were after a short and successful lifespan banned, on grounds that they protected the players too much. Schoolboys less as it were on the ball at games, subsequently stuffed books or clothes down their stockings while playing, which proved to be a beatable offence.

However, more obvious delineations in gameswear separated the men from the boys on the playing fields during this period. Football team members at Highgate School (1920s) were privileged to wear soft felt hats, although only for away matches, and the cricket team members were allowed boaters. Eton footballers (1920s) would wear quaint beaver hats on the field. However, privileges of team members at many schools were extended into other spheres of school life, and were often valued greatly. Sixth formers at Highgate School (1920s) who had distinguished themselves at games, could wear blue coats and grey trousers during the summer term, which made them the envy of the rest. Likewise, regular cyclists of Emanuel School at this period had the pleasure of exemption from having to wear boaters.

Accolades for distinction at games have remained an essential tradition of school uniform, varying from one era to the next in form bestowed but never in import.

Typical were the privileges extended to colours of Bristol Grammar School (1940s), to use the headmaster's lawn, and to take shortcuts to it

Captain of Rugby Football, Merchiston Castle School, Edinburgh, 1922.

Tennis players in pleated skirts, James Allen's Girls' School, London, 1920s.

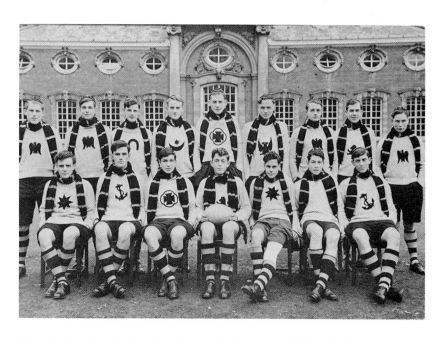

The rugby team, Wellington College, 1953. Note the house symbols on the jerseys.

by a spiral staircase. Colours of King's School, Rochester were until the 1950s permitted unorthodox town leave, and could patronise restaurants forbidden to the rest of the school.

The dress of colours and of the less privileged pupils came under the scrutiny of reformers. The familiar school plimsolls were criticised as follows by Salford's principal medical officer:

> These light canvas shoes not only give no support to the growing child but offer no protection from the weather, and offer free percolation of the dust and filth of the road through the uppers.

Although beloved by children, plimsolls did sometimes give rise to complaints even from that quarter. A pupil of Latymer Upper School attributed his failure to win a school race to the ill-fitting plimsolls he had worn in its duration, as it had transpired, another boy's.

Temporary relief from school uniform was still at hand, in the form of nude bathing at amongst other establishments Forest School, on which a former pupil there pronounces:

> Boots and socks were removed in the entrance, and then all other clothes discarded on the side of the bath. No one thought anything of this except a few new boys coming from small private schools, whose embarrassment at first caused a certain amount of amusement, but they all got used to the idea (they had to!) and we all gambolled together as unselfconscious as the unfallen Adam.

Such liberation at less privileged educational establishments was less frequently to hand. The boys of Sir Joseph Williamson's Mathematical School would go swimming in full one-piece black costumes, looking like so many black imps, and their instinct for modesty was indulged, perhaps at the expense of their comfort.

Even the most restrictive school uniform is remembered vividly by the old boys who had worn it in their day, and usually, although they may be loth to admit it, with a degree of nostalgia.

This nostalgia can find its catalyst in all sorts of unexpected places. A former pupil of Bedford School made an unexpected find on his travels in the Borneo forest, as he relates in this letter to the school magazine:

> Dear Sir,
>
> Please find enclosed evidence of old Bedfordian influence deep down inside East Kalimantan. I found the colours in a puddle in a Dayak village some two hundred miles up the Mahakan River on a recent expedition. There were no fine boats visible on the river, possibly because of the huge logs floating downstream; nor were there kayaks as might have been expected. Maybe John Osborne (Master of Rowing) had been looking further afield for competition? Any suggestions?
>
> Yours sincerely,
> Geoffrey Rockliffe King.

Just as old boys of the great public schools take the colours of their schooldays seriously, so do the new boys who are these institutions' bread and butter.

As is typical at many old public schools, the Headmaster of King's School, Rochester, regularly brings coloured squares in his mortar board to assembly, where he presents them to a chosen few, while the rest of the school claps madly, and cheers.

Indeed, colours at King's School, Rochester, elaborate in proportion to the seniority of the team to which the recipient belongs, become reproduced not just on these squares, but also on ties, on blazers, and on boater ribbons, at considerable expense to the boys' parents.

While such varied distribution of colours is the norm in many schools, there are alternative accolades, and prominent at schools such as the Grammar School, Bristol, Clifton College, Queen Elizabeth College, and St. Lawrence's, Ramsgate, is the much coveted house shield, which like colours, encourages the sort of corporate effort the great public schools have traditionally worked to encourage.

Within any school, teams matched against each other remain of course defined by distinctions in dress. These can be quite elaborate. Amongst players of the Eton Wall Game for instance, the side wearing black has jerseys, the side wearing white only shirts.

After the Eton Wall Game has been played before the public on St. Andrew's Day, all the participants appear drenched in a mudbath, making for difficulty in distinguishing sides. It is the Eton dame who bears the brunt of this, and one dame washed a player's shirt and socks eleven times, following which a maid gave them six more washes before sending them to the laundry.

Although a mudbath can be exciting for schoolboys, embarrassing situations remain less so. The love of school uniform is always full of new incidents involving uniforms' involuntary removal. When, for

Scholars v. Fee payers. The Eton Wall Game, 1963.

Armed to the teeth for hockey at Lawnside, Great Malvern, 1986.

instance, a class at Forge Lane Infants' School (1980s) stripped to underclothes for a gymnasium session, one boy climbed out of his underpants, believing this too was required, and a redfaced lady teacher promptly ushered him back into the changing room to the accompaniment of gales of laughter from his classmates of either sex.

Nudity can be genuinely imposed. In a rugger match between King's School, Rochester and Chatham Grammar School for Boys, one player's trousers were pulled off in a scrum. He had failed to wear underpants for the event, and for days after, could not live this down.

Removal of school uniform, problematic as it may on occasion be, is often easier than putting it on. Here is the fictional schoolboy Darbishire caught in a timehonoured dilemma of the school changing-rooms:

> 'It's these stupid boots,' replied Darbishire. 'My mother tied them together by the laces when she packed them, so's I wouldn't lose one without the other – not that I wanted to lose both'.

Like Darbishire, we must unravel the problem of gameswear, and, paying homage to our own experience of it back in our schooldays, as well as serving the interests of our progeny on the gamesfield, we must never let bygones be bygones.

Chapter 15

UNIFORM FOR ADULTS ONLY

School uniform, of natural interest to children, becomes an unnatural obsession with certain adults. The kind explanation for this is that it is the concrete symbol of schooldays which become ever more golden when looked back on through the mists of time.

It is indeed such nostalgia which fans the flames of old boys' clubs throughout the country, many of which do a roaring trade in adult versions of the old school uniforms.

These garments bearing the school colours are not supposed to be worn by any Tom, Dick or Harry, although they often actually are. Typically, the Old Emanuel Association in the 1930s complained that unauthorised persons had been seen wearing the old Emanuel School tie, but could do nothing about it.

More recently, the old boys' club of Sir Joseph Williamson's Mathematical School, Rochester, has arranged with Ogdens, the official school uniform retailer, that interested buyers must have their names recorded on a list of old boys. If pretentious, this practice bestows exclusivity, and so doubtless within its limited market bears commercial dividends. Furthermore, members of the public are denied access to dress enabling them to pose as old boys, which would appear sacrosanct to guardians of the 'Maths School' uniform.

The better known public schools do not attempt so much to safeguard exclusivity in their uniforms, which have been recognised as trend-setters amongst the population at large. Many a social climber has worn the Harrovian tie, or other items of Harrovian uniform, and such practice has been known to pay rich dividends in business, and in social life alike.

Also, imitation of uniform exclusive to the great public schools was rife, and the earliest chronicler of school uniform's history, the Reverend Wallace Clare, was intrigued to see an outfitter's advertisement for a bargain line in 'Eton suits with new sportsback' which appeared in an American journal. In tacit evocation of the original item, the blurb claimed: 'No other style can take its place. It's the traditional favourite'. Astutely, the new sportsback was not revealed in the illustration.

Of course many a genuine old boy has worn his old school tie, or other items of school dress in adult life. There is however, particularly amongst intelligentsia, a growing band of adults who recall the complex feelings for school uniform that they had harboured decades earlier, as wearers of it.

The author H.E. Bates for instance had as a small boy read the school magazine stories, and his old school, Kettering Grammar School, despite being geared to 'attempts at conformation with public school standards', didn't live up to his expectations, as he here explains:

> The masters certainly wore black gowns, but none of them had mortar boards and none of the boys wore bumstarvers.

However, old boys of more prestigious educational foundations may also nurture bitter memories of their schoolwear. In a speech to pupils of St. Paul's Boys' School, which he himself had once attended, Viscount Montgomery announced 'We (British) do not like uniforms', and his sentiments were doubtless not alien to his audience.

Indeed a former pupil of the sister school, the author Monica Dickens, recalls:

> I had got myself expelled from St. Paul's not only because I was fed up with the uniform hat, a black felt bucker like a Mennanite preacher, but I was fed up with brainwork.

Effective vindication may be less dramatic, as in the case of Henry Williamson, author of *Tarka the Otter*, whose highly critical novel *Dandelion Days* had a pseudonymous setting claimed to be akin to that of Colfe's Grammar School which Williamson himself had attended.

His descriptions of shabby unregulated schoolwear are enlightening for their period authenticity. A picture is painted of one boy wearing a

Henry Williamson, author of Tarka the Otter, *seated front row second right in this Colfe's School group at the Keston Field Club, 1910.*

The young Sir Thomas Beecham as a monitor (centre, with boater) at Rossall School, Fleetwood, Lancs, in this 1896 choir picture. Note the eccentric holding of hands and posture.

'threadworn Norfolk suit', distinctly of 'cheap materials'. His Eton collar is riddled with 'much mended stud-holes', and even his tie looks 'old'.

The example set by masters in Williamson's fictional school was not a happy one. Hear this description of the French master:

> Almost invariably, he wore a blue suit, shiny at the elbows. And the seat of his trousers was short, creaseless and baggy, with frayed bottoms.

Doubtless such exposition of dress contributed to the elevation of *Dandelion Days* to the status of required reading at one teachers' training college, on how not to run a school, as well as to a Colfeian obituary which pontificated: 'It is a pity that he (Williamson) apparently thought so little of his old school'.

Still less does the successsful children's author, Roald Dahl, think of the dress regulations in his own alma mater. In his autobiography *Boy,* he relates that when starting at Repton in his tailcoats, he felt like an 'undertaker's apprentice in a funeral parlour'. His wing collars were so tough that he felt obliged to chew them. He was even made to sit for fifteen minutes on the lavatory seat, with his trousers down, to warm it for a fagmaster.

Unlike Roald Dahl, the famous author George Orwell had refused to conform in the schools he had attended. His memoir of prep school focuses here on his dress:

> To this day I can feel myself swooning with shame as I stood a very small round faced boy in short corduroy knickers, before the two women.

Also a product of the private school system is the author Robert Graves. In his autobiography *Goodbye to All That,* he recalls the caste system, as pinpointed by the uniform at the Charterhouse School of his youth. The new boy, he notes, had to wait until his second term before he could wear a coloured tie. In his second year, he was permitted coloured socks, and in his third year he could turn down his collar, wear a coat with a long roll, and brandish a coloured handkerchief. In the senior school, there were other possibilities, as Graves here observes:

> The three sixth-formers walked slowly up the aisle, magnificent in light grey flannel trousers, slit jackets, butterfly collars, and each wore a pink carnation in his lapel.

The glories of such dress, enhanced as it is at school, become later lodged in certain adults' consciousness in the form of fetishes, which Dr Glenn Wilson has described as the 'immature emotion, to which people are ashamed to admit'. More optimistically, Helen Gardener argues that fetishism is a diversion, like angling or football, only superior insofar as it involves the opposite sex.

The school uniform fetish is of course one of the commonest kinds. In pornographic literature on the subject, schoolgirls are whipped and thrashed, with an essential preliminary being the drawn-out and depraved removal of their school uniform that symbolises innocence. Here is an extract from *Blushes,* in which the stern, bearded schoolmaster in a Scottish Presbyterian school prepares to cane a naughty female pupil.

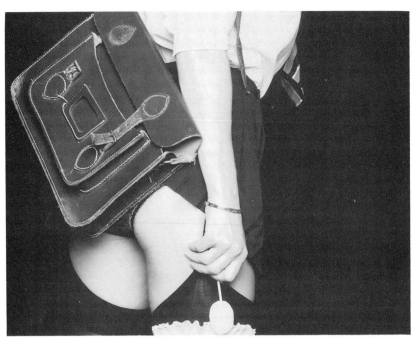

Suspenders with the soup from this waitress at School Dinners.

Lemmy of Motorhead making the most of his visit to School Dinners.

Fiona now weeping openly, stumbled towards the desk, pushing down her blue serge knickers. They reached her knees as she more or less fell across the desk, her hands clasping the far edge. Rather to Colin's surprise, Val Hildreth (another teacher) stepped forward and tucked the hem of Fiona's skirt up under her waistband.

Prominent amongst those who find this sort of writing a turn-on are upper class men, often with families, who remain fixated on the schoolgirl types who were their first objects of sexual interest.

Prostitutes too have captured this market, often through services involving school uniform. 'Schoolgirl in uniform', or 'Strict Governess gives French lessons to boys in uniform' are typical notices displayed with telephone numbers in newsagents' windows. Other notices such as: 'Paula's Academy for Naughty Boys' and 'Seats recaned, Miss Stern', whilst not directly referring to school uniform, nonetheless evoke it.

Uncatered for by the prostitutes are of course the paedophiles who sometimes lure schoolchildren with sweets, outside school gates or inside parks. Bright-eyed old men who fall into this category have invited schoolboys in uniform to 'have a pee' with them in the toilets of disreputable pubs.

This particular dirty mackintosh brigade has existed since time immemorial, and their one interest in school uniform lies in its removal. To this end the author Graham Greene as a child was invited by an elderly man he met in the park to visit his Scotland estate where all the guests wore kilts, 'so convenient in many ways'.

Still schoolboys at heart. An evening of nostalgia and fun at the restaurant School Dinners, *Baker Street, London.*

A waitress posing as a schoolgirl at School Dinners.

Not to be compared with this is the fun obsession with school uniform which flourishes in a comparatively subdued form amongst upright members of our society. Very popular amongst City gents is School Dinners, the central London restaurant. Here waitresses dressed like schoolgirls except for their black tights dole out school meals. In the background, a mock schoolmaster in gown and mortarboard flexes a cane. Customers are sent into the corner wearing a dunce's cap, and may be forced to do lines. This restaurant is often full.

One evening at School Dinners will give ex-public schoolboys in particular the most incredible nostalgic evening of their lives!

What a feast misty-eyed old boys are in for, as they scramble into the cellar restaurant whose walls are crammed with school photos, story book covers and other such tributes to the school classroom.

As you sit down at the table to order, for example, Matron's Secret Recipe and St. Trinian's Choice, service is provided by delightful young waitresses with striped ties, tight grey pleated skirts, half-cocked boaters and lacrosse sticks, who attend to every (reasonable) whim. They will even rebuke customers for sneaking, or for bad table manners. In the true school spirit PeePee the little black waiter dressed like a schoolboy, passes amongst the tables causing merriment.

The menu consists of nostalgic dishes such as apple crumble, spotty dick and all those old school favourites, only this time marvellously cooked and extremely appetising. Meanwhile the waitresses lean over the table suggestively, and crack naughty jokes.

But the real fun starts with a 'Headmaster's caning'. The hapless victim, usually a birthday boy or bridegroom-to-be on his stag night, is hauled before the 'Headmaster' – School Dinners' general manager in a mortar board and gown.

He is bent over and given a mock caning by two 'schoolgirl' waitresses, while the Headmaster beats a gong to accompany every stroke. The caning last long and appears hard. The diners – ex-public school City people, and, increasingly others, are in a seventh heaven! What a delicious trip down memory lane this is! Of course, it is fun, not real perversion, and many business deals are swung in this atmosphere. At no other London restaurant is there such imaginative live theatre!

The commercial success of this unique venture bears testimony to the importance of school uniform in our national culture, often surpassing that of any other uniform, as author Jan Morris has discovered the hard way, relating here how much more terrifying he had found the Lancing College Cadet Corps than the British army:

> For twenty years or more I dreamt about the horror of those parades, and of the burning pale blue eyes of the cadet sergeant, approaching the expectant and mocking down the ranks.

A hard time with school uniform for very different reasons was had by a pupil at Charterhouse School, described by his contemporary, the author Simon Raven, as 'poor stupid Holby' who got into a 'positively fetishist state' about his uniform. His eagerness to dress correctly was such that he scrounged garments not only from masters and parents, but even from the school museum.

Perhaps a healthier reaction to school uniform is to take it with a pinch of salt, and author William Boyd is reminded of an old schoolfriend who had worn his school dufflecoat like a cloak, to emulate his hero, Oscar Wilde.

Such humour may ease the national obsession with school uniform, but it will never annihilate it, and school uniform will always have its place in the lives of adults.

Chapter 16

UNIFORM TO PLEASE OUR MAKER

The sober colours and non sensual feel of school uniform throughout the ages owes much to the influence of the various churches. School founders have been known to be religious fanatics, and Edward Alleyn, the famous actor who founded Dulwich College in 1617, was by one reliable account:

> So equally mingled with humility and charity that he became his own pensioner, humbly submitting himself to the proportion of diet and cloathes which he had bestowed on others.

Most exciting for the children were rituals of pagan origin. Girls of Deptford Boarding School in 1617, in a masque called 'Cupid's Banishment' which they performed at Greenwich Palace in front of Queen Anne, wore white flowers in their hair, much to the encouragement of the boys who were in fact acting most of the parts.

Less popular was the standard seventeenth century Christ's Hospital uniform, whose pious origins became highlighted right up to the 1850s by a custom here stipulated by Edward Arris in 1669, as a condition of his bequeathing £6.00 per annum to the school:

> 240 boys, each of them to have a pair of white gloves, and everyone of them to wear a paper with these words on it, videlicet, in great letters. "He is risen", and this is to be done upon Easter Sunday, Monday, Tuesday, and Wednesday, and the paper visibly to be seen.

Nonetheless, the wearing of this and of other uniforms with religious origins was enforced with cast iron discipline, particularly in boarding schools where there was often no relapse into less formal wear.

In the great Catholic schools on the continent during the seventeenth century, boys were cooped up for years at a stretch, due to rigorous persecutions of Catholics at home, and all the time they had to wear their soutanes.

Discarding the soutane, although a novel experience, was necessary when venturing into the world. Even the pedagogic religious orders recognised this, and the caring Father Garan said of St. Omers boys:

> When they go out, they go in secular clothes, that none might know when any person leaves the college.

So conditioned to wear their uniforms were the St. Omers boys that during the fraught period of the French Revolution, some travelled to England fully clad in their ecclesiastical garb, and it caused them to be taken for Frenchmen.

Evidently then, boys of this period in the Catholic Schools took pride in their soutanes, but they still craved to assert their individuality

Catholic boys at Douai School, Berks, 1881-82.

through their dress. Some wore ribbons in hats coloured to suit themselves, whilst others selected what buckles they wore, as this account from eighteenth century Downside demonstrates:

> A pair of silver buckles for Mr. Swinburne, £1.1s.0d.
> A pair of plated buckles for Mr. Throckmorton, 3s.6d.
> A pair of silver buckles for Mr. Bodenham, 15s.

Such variety enhanced children's pride in their school uniform, and it seemed natural at the Quaker schools that the female pupils should become involved in its manufacture. For instance, at the Friends' School, Saffron Walden (1728), with its workhouse foundation, the arrival of a new boy, Scipio Africanus, meant work for the girls, and the fact that he was black definitely didn't diminish their zeal. Materials were bought to make his coat, his waistcoat, and his breeches, as well as yarn to knit into further clothes for his use, while Scipio's hat, gloves, buckles and a 'black periwig' would be bought from outside, along with knife, fork, spoon, and 'an ivory comb'.

Scipio Africanus, like other pupils of Quaker schools, became clad in plain and durable clothes that gave no indication of financial means.

The enforcement of such schoolwear, in allegiance to the Quaker doctrine, remained rigid throughout the ages. Typically, at Sidcot School, Winscombe, in 1810, the Superintendent was duty-bound 'to report to the committee if any striking deviation from plainness and simplicity appeared in clothing sent by the children'. In this spirit, Sidcot School pupils who grew out of their uniform were issued with standardised replacements.

Although it gave rise to few complaints, Sidcot School's uniform was neither comfortable nor attractive. The only undergarment in issue was a dowlas shirt, so stiff that it would stand up of its own accord when not on a pupil's torso. Hats and shoes alike, purchased wholesale, proved ill-fitting. One pupil described her hat as 'inflexible dog-hair, hard enough on the head'. Girls' frocks were replaced with ugly brown dresses made on the premises, and their straw bonnets were deprived of trimmings.

Eccentric innovations in uniform would sometimes bring a much needed comfort. A basket of nightcaps started being carried round bedrooms at Sidcot School, so boys could keep their heads warm, and they welcomed this opportunity. A black gown, phased in in 1849 to be worn all day long over other clothes, was gratifying for its looseness.

Of course, not all innovations were accepted so readily. Uniquely at Sidcot School (1850), boys started wearing on the arms of their gowns the initials H.C. stitched in red, standing for 'highest class', until a few astute rebels spread the word that it stood for 'half cracked' which led promptly to this motto's abolition.

It was rebels too at Francis Holland School (1897) who, in defiance of the school's Christian ethos, during hockey matches 'kept the ball too much under their petticoats', for which they were punished by being made to wear longer skirts.

Rebels, unless purely in spirit, are given simply no chance at the fictional Loward School, whose master Mr Brocklehurst, in this extract from Charlotte Bronte's classic novel *Jane Eyre*, enunciates:

Juniors of St. Leonards-Mayfield School, 1886. Note the distinctive frilled bonnets.

Sidcot School pageant, 1935, in which the girls appear in 1809 Quaker dress.

The Clothes List, 1808, as represented in the Sidcot School pageant, 1935.

> I have a master to serve whose kingdom is not of this world: my mission is to
> mortify in these girls the lusts of the flesh, to teach them to clothe themselves
> with shamefacedness and sobriety, not with braided hair and costly apparel.

It hardly comes as a surprise that Casterton, the real life school on which
Loward was based, forced its pupils, who were mostly daughters of
clergymen, to wear a uniform so hideous that Dorothea Beal, the
renowned educational reformer who taught there for a year, developed
from this experience her personal distaste for uniform.

For the familiar reason of piety, school uniform worn in convents has
traditionally been unattractive. At many convents, patent leather shoes
were forbidden, lest girls should admire themselves in the sheen, which
would constitute the sin of pride.

Rituals of dress in convents were often more directly sanctimonious, as
for instance was the pupils' widespread custom of crossing their
stockings over a neatly folded bundle of clothes, prior to going to sleep.

Far more restrictive, due to its punitive purpose, was the wearing of
tight gloves as a penalty for biting nails or pinching, and pupils in
convents regarded this as a nightmare punishment.

Relief was however to come to girls of some convents, in the form of a
young man who visited regularly to shampoo their hair, on which
occasions they could relieve their necks of high starched collars, a treat
indeed.

Less exciting but treasured by the more dutiful convent girls were the
bright ribbons awarded for unnaturally good conduct. Obviously such
ribbons repelled the rebels, and indeed two girls at one convent sported
red ribbons on St. Patrick's Day to challenge the green ribbons which the
Irish hockey team wore in accordance with tradition. The offenders,
rebuked at school assembly by an hysterical nun, nonetheless had the
last laugh, finding, when they returned to the school as old girls in later
years, that the custom of the English wearing red ribbons on St. Patrick's
Day had taken root and flourished.

Not just ribbons but other trivial items of schoolwear assumed a
symbolic significance in convents, which at times has reached almost
mystical proportions. Girls would dress in Sunday best and special
'cachet' shoes for the 'Cachet Ceremony', in which form marks and
conduct reports would be presented to them in an assembly, before the
rest of the school. The pupils' sense of occasion was certainly enhanced
by their dress.

More revered than cachet shoes and Sunday best was the nun's habit
and wimple. Generations of schoolgirls delighted in seeing a nun's wisp
of greying hair peeping from under a wimple, and would speculate as to
what the full head of hair looked like.

For pupils themselves to don the habit and wimple was a dream that
came true for 'Children of Mary' at Holy Child Convent, St. Leonard's-
on-Sea (1940s) on St. Teresa's Day, when thus dressed like nuns, they
would even take classes.

All pupils in this convent and not just the 'Children of Mary' were
granted the privilege of being able to hang stockings outside the curtains

of their bedroom cubicles, which meant they would be left to lie in of a morning. If they omitted to do this, a nun at 6.30 a.m. would pull aside the curtain and say: 'Blessed be the Holy Child Jesus'. Should the sleepy pupil not reply 'Now and forever more, Amen', the nun would strip off the girl's bedclothes, and maybe even her nightie.

Into the 1950s, dress regulations in convents remained strict. At the Sacred Heart Convent, Hammersmith, for example, nuns would whip out tape measures at unexpected moments, and would check that girls' skirts were of the correct length. Big Sister was watching all pupils.

Even in this era, most would not dream of rebelling too openly. A pupil of St. Joseph's, Abbey Wood (1950s) who resented the maroon kippers she was forced to wear there, prayed for high-heeled shoes, which if less sensible and comfortable, would at least have been fashionable. She never, however, got as far as wearing them.

Some of her contemporaries, in the same deferential spirit, opted not to wear the attractive summer dress available to them, so as to avoid the sin of vanity. One pupil secretly wore forbidden frilly knickers for three nerve-racking months, until she felt unable to face the risk of discovery any longer, and took to wearing the sober regulation knickers. Overall, the nuns of St. Joseph's had done their work well.

In order to instil such guilt, the nuns have had to punish miscreants rigorously, as is demonstrated in this extract from Clare Boylan's novel *Holy Pictures,* where a naughty convent girl who has hitched up her gymslip must pay the price:

> 'I will tell you,' Mother Ignatius said softly as if she had some important confidence to impart, 'Your legs are nothing to be proud of. Now, see how you like going round for the rest of the day like this!' She fell painfully to her knees and began pinning sheets of newspaper around the abbreviated hem.

In recent years, the popularity of stripping nuns to celebrate birthdays and other special occasions in City offices particularly has represented to some extent a belated revenge on the strict schoolmarm nun of yesteryear. Indeed, this species of strippogram has been known to sing of undressing in the girls' dormitories, to great applause.

Naturally, pupils in schools have less blind a reverence for the religious orders. A pupil of Sion Convent (1970s) felt a frisson to witness a respected nun slip on a step, and so tread on her habit, defiling it. A pupil of another convent would stick pins in her lifelike sketches of nuns. One parent observed a monk of Ampleforth Abbey (1980s) raising his habit to protect his head from the pelting rain as he stumbled across the moors on a stormy day.

Schoolteachers of the religious orders sometimes now work in mufti, which means that such a nun will no longer get up from her chair only to have ground chalk blotching her behind with the devastating conspicuousness that was traditionally her fate. No longer do pupils walk in dread of the gloomy portrait of the foundress nun who may be appearing to eye them malevolently from inside her frame.

Today's educational environment, comparatively liberal in its demands for uniformity of dress, has been influenced by the ideas of

Choristers of St. John's College School, Cambridge crossing The Bridge of Sighs in their gowns and mortar boards.

St. John's College School pupils wearing scarlet blazers identical to those worn by the oarsmen of the St. John's College Boat Club who whilst rowing down the river Cam, appeared to be ablaze on the water. This incident gave the word 'blazer' to the English language.

A.S. Neill, the pioneer Headmaster of Summerhill School, where pupils shed their clothes at will, sitting around shirtless if they please. A.S. Neill here states:

> Religion as I remember it, practised by men and women in drab clothes, singing mournful hymns of tenth rate music, asking forgiveness for their sins – this is nothing I wish to be identified with.

Liberalism has extended to choir schools, where ordinary schoolwear is sometimes worn. Choristers of St. Paul's Cathedral School for instance dress in modest grey trousers and dark blazers. The school secretary has commented: 'We have our work cut out getting them to wear pullovers'. On special occasions however, such as upon the Queen Mother's visit to the Cathedral, they wear smart Eton suits. What a contrast this makes.

Likewise dressed for best, pupils of King's College Choir School, Cambridge wear not just Eton suits, but even top hats to boot. Still more sumptuous is formal dress for pupils of St. John's College Choir School, consisting of academic gowns in the Cambridge University style, and red blazers of the Lady Margaret Boating Club, as worn by the St. John's College, Cambridge rowing team, once described as 'ablaze on the river Cam', which epithet gave the word 'blazer' to the English language.

Pupils of other Oxford and Cambridge College choir schools are likewise smartly dressed. They may be flaunting mortarboards, bowlers or caps. Wing or Eton collars are as likely to be worn as soft ones. Black ties are also characteristic.

Indeed in choir schools where pious appearance of school uniform is paramount, time seems to have stood still. No less traditional and spectacular than the uniforms described above are the long stockings, the breeches buckled just below the knee, the white bands, and the distinctive coats worn by choristers of the Chapel Royal. Conspicuous too is the royal red of Westminster Abbey Choir School.

More scholarly is the appearance of choristers of King's School, Rochester, in their mortar boards and their red or blue cassocks, complete with surplices.

King's Scholars of this school wear mortar boards too, and in the case of the head King's Scholar, with a distinctive blue tassel attached.

Smart in a more familiar style are the Queen's Scholars of Westminster School, in their headwaiter style morning coats, their white bow ties and surplices.

Religious influence in dress may vanish in schools without cathedral traditions, or other religious foundation. Hence, Jewish boys at non-denominational schools dispense with skull caps. Interestingly, however, Sikh boys retain their turbans, sometimes in place of motorcycle helmets, and other committed members of non-Christian faiths will similarly assert themselves.

Religion is perhaps the most formative influence on school uniform, and does much to keep it alive in these secular times.

Chapter 17

UNIFORM AT FIRST REMOVE

Lower uniform was removed layer by layer in the ritual preceding a public flogging at the great public schools during the Victorian era, and this practice achieved its purpose of both shocking the schoolboy onlookers and thoroughly embarrassing the victims. The ceremony was rarely done in private.

At Eton College for instance, the victim knelt down on the block with his trousers down, and two boys would hold up his shirt tails throughout execution, while the rest of the school was watching.

This denuding of pupils could of course backfire. One Etonian, about to be flogged, arranged for a picture of the Headmaster to be painted on his buttocks. The flogger, upon lifting his shirt, found himself as it were looking in the mirror. As the story goes, he erased all traces of the picture with the application of two birches.

The more elaborate the initial process of removing uniform, the more mystical was the aura which enveloped public school floggings. At Winchester, this ritual was more sophisticated than at Eton, and involved the victim kneeling while one boy unbuckled his braces, and another held up his shirt, exposing the small of his back.

In such floggings, and in corporal punishment of schoolchildren generally, it is the removal of underpants that embarrasses them most. One self-styled old Etonian and expert on beating of this era argued: 'Any interposition of underclothing materially interferes with the efficiency of the operation'. On the other hand, a highly successful contemporary proprietor of a cane-selling business, Eric Huntingdon, argued: 'We do not advocate the use of the cane on bare flesh. Pants afford the modesty a child is entitled to'.

Into the twentieth century, school beatings involving the baring of flesh became rarer. Dress regulations were still enforced rigidly in some schools, but light relief was sometimes not so distant. A former pupil of Bradford Girls' Grammar School (1920s) recalls here partaking in an early school debate:

> We held it in the art room, with Miss Morton in the chair, and a handsome, slender Denis Healey, proposing the motion, threw a brief glance at Venus de Milo and said he was glad that at least one girl had escaped the stringencies of school uniform.

All pupils, however, here and in other schools, had their opportunity to discard school uniform briefly when they used the lavatory cubicles. There was more to these than met the eye. The cubicle doors at Malvern

The parting gift: Dr. Warre's retirement from Eton, 1905, as sketched by Sidney P. Hall MVO.

for instance had no locks. Still worse was the situation at The College, Winchester, whose lavatory cubicles were not even equipped with doors. One renowned old boy, Tim Brooke-Taylor, comments:

> I defy anyone to be totally relaxed with their trousers round their ankles, within sight of what seems to be the whole world.

Of course, pupils' own removal of their uniform can be less temporary. George Macdonald Fraser has this to say of his first day at public school:

> My drooping garments excited coarse comment... I tore off those beastly drawers and hurled them into the River Kelvin.

Peer pressure in this context is a typical influence, but uniform may be removed on occasions for more esoteric purposes. Boys of the Oratory Preparatory School (1970s) would sometimes practise levitation at night, elevating a naked pupil by torchlight, to great effect, although to what extent defiance of gravity took place is debatable.

Pupils' commitment to rituals involving removal of school uniform has been matched only by that of their teachers, as the liberal 1960s were starting to show. A 1967 Home Office inquiry revealed that one Headmaster had been in the habit of pulling out boys' shirts before caning their buttocks, a ritual which could not have been necessary. Meanwhile, cases involving divestment of school uniform for purposes of child abuse were rife. Schoolmaster, William Byrd, was in 1968 sentenced to five years' imprisonment for 'gratifying his own sadistic urges' by stripping boys and caning them. Another teacher was imprisoned for photographing cartwheeling schoolgirls with their legs awry, offering a full view of regulation knickers. Many teachers have made girls in their charge pregnant, or interfered disgustingly with pupils in their charge, and some such cases have remained unreported.

In this context, the propriety demanded of teachers has led to their turning a blind eye on decadent rituals involving removal of school uniform practised by the pupils themselves. Birthday boys at St. Benedict's, Ealing (1970s) would have their trousers pulled down by the rest, and hung on the flagpole overlooking the school playground. The hapless victim, sprinting in his underpants across the concrete, would have to haul down his trousers himself. This was of course the age of streaking, and the introduction of girls into the sixth form only added to the thrills.

Games masters, while not sanctioning little games of this kind, have traditionally supervised boys taking showers in the nude after playing school sport.

In these school shower rooms, sadism has often enough been known to rear its ugly head. Any items of uniform may be used as a lethal weapon, including the school towel. In this extract from Barry Hines' novel *Kes*, the schoolboy Billy Casper tries to escape from the cold shower the gamesmaster, Sugden, has forced on him:

> Billy tried another rush. Sugden repelled it, so he tried the other end. Every time he tried to escape the three boys bounced him back, stinging him with their snapping towels as he retreated. He tried manoeuvring the nozzles, but

whichever way he twisted them the water still found him out, until finally he gave up, and stood among them, tolerating the freezing spray in silence.

As in the shower rooms, so in the Headmaster's study, still occasionally the locale for canings. But today's pupils, when subject to beatings without having to take their trousers down, know how to defend themselves. Here is Nigel Molesworth of St. Custard's relating his experiences as described in *Down with Skool*:

> Tiptoe shuffle shuffle zoom down on Fotherington-tomas and shave his curly locks. While he blubs i stuff the locks inside my trousis.
> Go to study. Kane descend whack gosh so gosh so gosh and hares fly out like H-bomb explosion. Kane undamaged so it is not such a wizard wheeze after all, but Headmaster gets a piece of his wife's mind (making mess after maids hav been in). So BOYS triumphant agane WIZZ.

Pupils also gain the upper hand, if at virtually no other time, during the holidays. Here are some convent girls temporarily free of school, as described in *A temple of the Holy Ghost*, a short story by Flannery O'Connor:

> They came in the brown convent uniforms they had to wear at Mount St. Scholastica, but as soon as they opened their suitcases, they took off the uniforms and put on red skirts and loud blouses. They put on lipstick and their Sunday shoes and walked around in the high heels all over the house.

Some pupils wait until their early adult years to ditch their school uniforms, and then do it with vigour. The universities are crammed with ex-public school rebels lounging about in filthy jeans and T-shirts, a habit some never kick.

Others get their thrills from recreating their old school uniform rituals in sexual games that prove their mastery over what had once mastered them.

In this context, one correspondent to *Forum* has told of his kinky practices as a twelve year old schoolboy. With his partner, he had indulged in the 'usual tortures and initiations', clad in only pyjama tops and tight underpants. Next had come schoolboy spanking sessions using that *sine qua non* of school uniform, the gymslipper.

Inevitably, even the dullest school uniform, if frustrating its wearers, will likewise protect them. Herodotus, the famous historian of Ancient Greece, once quipped that too full a clothing of the body was a sign of weakness. This may be so, but are not children by definition weak?

Chapter 18

A HARDWEARING INVESTMENT

Buying school uniform in the period between the wars was a pleasurable experience. In this era, the department stores which stocked it had reached an acme of luxury and of usefulness. They served as a haven for weary shoppers.

Likewise, school uniform was at a peak of popularity. There was a proliferation of major schools, as well as of small boarding schools, and they all had specific schoolwear requirements, so the demand was voluminous. Families would come from some distance to London, and to major provincial cities such as Liverpool and Manchester to fit out their children, taking advantage of their visits to make purchases over and above those of school uniform.

Such customers, when temporarily fatigued, could sink into chairs distributed throughout the store for their convenience. Meanwhile, assistants in generous number would stand by, offering tactful suggestions, and shopwalkers would patrol departments, watching and guiding customers as well as staff.

All this was symptomatic of the big business that the school uniform industry was generating, and naturally the profits were considerable. The prosperous middle class families in particular would visit the stores to buy uniform several times a year. Furthermore, since boys' and girls' school uniform departments were strictly segregated, and often located on different floors, families with children at separate schools would often make two visits to the store during the summer holidays.

An abundance of schoolwear was bought in one swoop, to comply with school clothing lists that were by modern standards formidable, including not just uniforms as such, but also underwear, games kits, sheets, blankets, eiderdowns, even rugs. Normally, several of each item were needed, so for instance a child would typically be equipped with six pairs of regulation knickers, twelve pairs of socks, four pairs of pyjamas, and four pairs of sheets, along with extras such as a school trunk. The expense of all this was daunting, even by the standards of the day.

The summer term brought still further expense, with the issuing of a supplementary clothing list which would include such items as summer vests, shirts, blouses, regulation swimming costumes, and tennis rackets. Some parents were forced to economise as much as they dared here, a ploy which found little favour with Headteachers.

So prolific were these school clothing lists, that frequently several stores used to supply uniform for one school, which meant competition

An advertisement for St. Paul's evening dress, Gooch's of Knightsbridge, 1937.

Daniel Neal's advertisement for gingham school frocks that never shrink or fade.

was fierce. The main London stores were John Lewis, Selfridges, Harrods and William Whiteley, but there were others in the provinces such as Lewis's of Liverpool.

Although it was not, strictly speaking, a department store, the famous Daniel Neal posed formidable competition in its provision of school uniform.

Daniel Neal was a vast shop in Portman Square, with a satellite branch in Kensington High Street. The shop was entirely devoted to provision of children's clothes.

Its interior was divided into departments: Baby Linen, Party Clothes, Shoes, and most significantly, Boys' School Uniform and Girls' School Uniform. Mothers and nannies who shopped here for the new term were certainly tempted by the new party dresses or the smart winter coats. Daniel Neal thrived right into the 1960s, when the John Lewis Partnership took it over.

In addition to these famous retailers, London had its share of small specialist shops, in particular Plums in Victoria Street, where the Westminster boys bought their own esoteric uniform, Billings and Edmonds who are still supplying the smartest prep schools, and Rowes of Bond Street, also specialising in prep school uniforms, as well as in high quality children's leisure wear.

Small uniform suppliers flourished in the provinces, meeting uniform needs for local day schools. The lists were less demanding than those of

Lewis's of Liverpool making the most of the advertising potential of their hat brushes.

Outfits to suit the occasion

Equipping a boy for the many and varied sides
of his life can be a complicated business—expensive
too, unless very carefully planned.
To help you get the right answer for the right
occasions, and for the minimum outlay, much of our school
age clothing at Daniel Neal's is made in "Collegiate",
"Popular" and "Knockabout" grades with variations in
finish and cost.   But each grade gives sterling wear for
the particular need, however robust it may be.
Look through these pages to see the value
offered in clothing and footwear, then come in to one
of our stores and let our experts advise you.

Daniel Neal's

LONDON   ·   BOURNEMOUTH   ·   BRISTOL   ·   CHELTENHAM   ·   EXETER

NO HOLING OUT WITH THESE GUARANTEED SOCKS

Boys are notoriously heavy on socks and, normally, holes seem to develop within an incredibly short space of time.

We are sure that the answer to this problem lies in our hosiery specially made from a mixture of 50% nylon and 50% wool.

Our confidence is so great that we give a **GUARANTEE OF SIX MONTHS** normal wear without darning. If holes do appear within that time we will gladly replace the pair free of charge.

C509. Ankle socks in grey. Foot sizes 7½-8½″ **5/6**; 9-10½″ **5/11**

C627. Three-quarter hose in grey. Foot sizes 7½-9½″ **7/9**; 10-10½″ **8/3**

C556. Half-hose in grey or white. Foot size 10-11½″ **7/3**

C540. Half-hose in new short style, with Lastex tops. In grey or white. Foot sizes 10-11½″ **6/11**

"VIYELLON"

C641. Grey three-quarter hose in the new 'Viyellon' wool and nylon blend by the makers of Viyella. Also guaranteed against darning within six months of purchase or replaced free of charge. Foot sizes 7½-8″ **8/11**; 8½-9½″ **9/11**; 10″ **10/11**

2

Pages from Daniel Neal's school uniform catalogue, 1957.

School Suits in medium grey

A635
A630

A167, A162

TROUSER SUITS

"Popular" wool/nylon flannel suit with self-supporting trousers. A635 (*above, left*). Sizes 7-8 **155/-**; 9-10 **162/6**; 11-12 **177/6**; 13-14 **185/-**

"Collegiate" suit with two-button jacket, all worsted melange flannel. A629 (*not illustrated*) Sizes 7-8 **195/-**; 9-10 **205/-**; 11-12 **225/-**; 13-14 **235/-**

"Knockabout" suit in hardwearing fibro and wool mixture with a fine worsted appearance. A630 (*illustrated as A635 above, left*). Sizes 7-8 **135/-**; 9-10 **140/-**; 11-12 **150/-**

KNICKER SUITS

"Popular" wool/nylon flannel knicker suit. Shorts are unlined but have double seats. A167 (*centre*). Sizes 0-2 **85/-**; 3-5 **92/6**; 6-8 **100/-**

"Collegiate" suit with two-button jacket in all-worsted melange flannel. Lined shorts. A164 (*not illustrated*). Sizes 0-2 **110/-**; 3-5 **120/-**; 6-8 **130/-**

"Knockabout" knicker suit in hardwearing fibro and wool mixture with a worsted appearance. A162 (*above, right*). Sizes 3-5 **77/6**; 6-8 **81/-**

3

boarding schools. It was the parents' business how many pairs of socks their child possessed.

Still, the requirements seem excessive to us today. Commonly needed for footwear, for instance, were indoor shoes, outdoor shoes, plimsolls, games shoes, dancing pumps, summer sandals, and Wellington boots with special socks to go inside them.

All items taken to day or boarding schools had to be marked with Cash's nametapes, which were ordered through the uniform supplier. They are still available, but marking ink has become the cheaper, lazier alternative.

Just as the use of nametapes has declined, so since the Second World War has exclusive uniform been increasingly confined to a few garments, a typical example being expensive blazers, as worn with Marks & Spencers trousers.

Despite children's pleas for fashionable schoolwear, Headteachers' demands that uniform should be practical and respectable have overruled this, and styles have changed surprisingly little since the Second World War.

The blazer in prewar years made of wool that would so easily wear out, has however become more robust. In the 1970s, some twenty years after nylon was introduced for girls' skirts, polyester was introduced for the blazer, which made it significantly more hardwearing.

Nowadays the blazer is slimmer than it was, generally with a two button fastening as opposed to three button, and with a narrower lapel

Lewis's of Liverpool's window display to celebrate the store's 90th anniversary.

width of some two inches. It is usually now made from washable material, either 100% polyester, or polyester viscose filament yarn.

As demand for school uniform has declined, so have the great department stores. Not only are they no longer particularly luxurious but many have closed down, challenged or ousted by chain stores such as Marks & Spencers, British Home Stores, and Littlewoods. In very recent times, the out of town hypermarkets have added to the competition.

Blatantly, local shopping malls such as that in Brent Cross have obviated the necessity for people to make mammoth shopping expeditions to the West End, and high fares have added to this trend.

It is inevitable, granted school uniform has become so much less special, and less formal into the bargain, that a new category of standardised uniform, now acceptable at very many schools, has become available in every chain store. Typical items incorporated in it are trousers or pleated skirts of grey terylene, grey pullovers, striped or plain grey jerseys, white shirts, striped or checked summer dresses.

Parents approve such semi uniform because it is available locally, is well made, and above all, is reasonably priced. Children too tolerate it better than the more specialist stuff, which it is known they often resent. Some convent girls in Liverpool for instance hate their uniforms so much that they won't let their parents buy it, and back at school will pretend the missing items were out of stock. The nuns ring up Lewis's, the local

BOYS' TAILORING.

THE "*MOSCOW*" SUIT.

This Suit is the most stylish and suitable for Boys from 8 to 13 years of age. Made in useful Tweeds, Deerskins, Meltons, and a variety of strong materials, for School and better wear, in prices from 12/6 for the first size up to 21/-. Also in Black and Blue Worsteds, Diagonals, Satarras, Fancy Worsteds, Silk Mixtures, etc., at prices ranging from 18/- to 35/-.

Made in the following sizes :
Size 3 4 5 6 7 8 9
To fit Boys aged 8 9 10 11 12 13 14 years.

Lewis's Great Establishment in Ranelagh St.,
Liverpool.

BOYS' TAILORING.

THE "*RANELAGH*" SUIT.

This Suit is the most gentlemanly that can be worn by Youths from 11 to 17 years of age. It is made in good, sound, strong Tweeds, Meltons, Deerskins, Serges, etc., from 14/6 to 32/-. Also in Fancy Silk Mixtures, Black, Blue, and Grey Worsteds, Black and Blue Satarras, Diagonals, etc., from 20/- upwards.

Made in the following sizes :
Size 7 8 9 10 11 11½
To fit Youths aged 11 12 13 14 15 16½ years.

Lewis's Great Establishment in Ranelagh St.,
Liverpool.

Two of Lewis's styles, as advertised in the Victorian boys' novelette The Miller in His Men, *published by that firm.*

A Victorian advertisement issued by Lewis's of Liverpool.

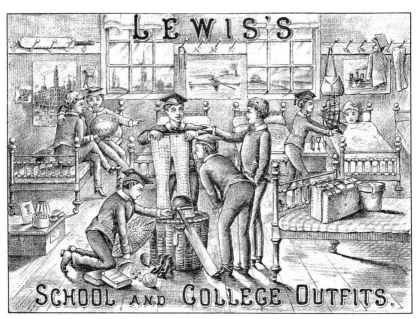

Lewis's of Liverpool never missed an advertising opportunity, as evidenced by these advertisements in an 1886 penny Shakespeare.

Ian Thomas (right) and Robert Seaborne (left) of school outfitters Eric Thomas & Co (Sidcup) Ltd looking smart in their blazers and boaters.

department store at all hours of the day and night to check their stories, and, sadly, as a sales supervisor points out, the store cannot afford to protect the girls.

However retailers of school uniform cannot afford to ignore children's fads, and will steer a tricky middle course between fashion and practicality. On the one hand they will stock the popular brand names which may be of inferior quality, and cost more, but which the children will push their mothers into buying. As one retailing manager puts it: 'If schoolgirls will only buy split miniskirts, we have to provide them or we'd go out of business.' On the other hand, retailers will visit schools regularly, and check that Headteachers are happy with uniform, also giving out free calendars, organising display evenings, and otherwise publicising their services. Sympathetic and patient sales assistants serve the customers in the shop, the best assistants being middle-aged women who understand parents' needs.

If retailers ever become less than diligent, Headteachers may withdraw their business, sometimes when the forthcoming year's uniform has already been ordered. The subsequent losses will just have to be borne. As one retailer puts it: 'If we took schools to court, no Headteacher in the country would ever use us.'

To keep in schools' good books, retailers must quickly provide uniform in all shapes and sizes. Recently, one retailer, ordering a large pair of school shorts, put in his letter for the benefit of the cutter: 'Please note – this boy has a backside like a baking of bread.'

As well as being infinitely flexible in its dimensions, school uniform must prove tough to survive the rigours not just of school life, but of being handed down to siblings for a no less hard second lease of life.

The retailers, working in liaison with reliable manufacturers, are surviving in today's tough competitive market-place, but are sometimes forced to shoulder responsibility for their own product, for its strengths and its weaknesses, even though they provide only to order.

To some extent, this protects the schools. As one Headteacher puts it: 'Thank God adolescents make school uniform their target, otherwise they'd all be getting at us more instead.'

Chapter 19

GLOSSARY

Academic Gown
See Gown.
Beret
A round, flat or felt cloth cap, worn by schoolgirls. This is sometimes red, but is frequently more conservatively coloured. Berets have often been thrown about, and had their tassels pulled off by rebellious schoolgirls.
Bloods
These are members of public schools' leading sports teams, and are usually privileged. For example, bloods at Marlborough College (1920s) were allowed to carry around silk handkerchiefs.
Bloomers
An outmoded and cumbersome women's undergarment with loose, knee-length trousers. Bloomers were frequently coloured a garish pink.
Blue Book
A traditional book of precise, often pedantic regulations, often relating to dress, at the King's School, Canterbury. There have been recent, controversial attempts at reviving these rules.
Bluer (Harrow)
The blue flannel coat worn by all boys going to 'footer', or in the summer to cricket.
Boater
A hard flat straw hat, as once worn by boating parties. In the nineteenth century boaters were adopted by orphanages, and were consequently given up by the socially self-conscious. Despite this set-back, boaters retain snob-value and are still worn at some schools, if mostly for special occasions.
Bot-pads
Large cushions that boys of Bishop's Stortford College used to take into class. When they started using them as missiles, bot-pads were abolished (1927).
Brassiere
Once a sleeveless nightshirt for men and women, this was reintroduced in its modern form by Paul Poiret in 1912.
Breeches
Short trousers, usually fastened below the knee, worn by nineteenth century schoolchildren.
Bumbags
An epithet used earlier this century for ordinary swimming trunks at Eton College and at Charterhouse School.

Bumfreezers
Eton jackets (q.v.).

Butterfly collars
Raised collars, as worn by pupils of The King's School, Canterbury, on the principle that pride must be pinched. These are comfortable only when they fit well. Also called stick-up or wing collars.

Cachet Ceremony
The presentation of form marks and of conduct reports to individuals before the entire school, a nerve racking experience for pupils. This was normal in some convents.

Cap (Harrow)
To 'cap' a master is to touch the cap to him. A 'cap' is a cap of house colours which is given by captains of house cricket elevens to members of the house eleven.

Cathedrals (cathers)
The word for 'top hats' at Winchester.

Choristers
Children who sing for their school, and who have passed a competitive exam to qualify for this.

Christ's Hospital Style
Dress based on the original Christ's Hospital uniform, featuring a blue cassock still worn there. The Christ's Hospital style, with minor variations is still worn at several charity schools, in most cases only on special occasions.

Clothing coupons
Tokens issued in wartime to buy clothes. Allowances were made for children's growth.

Coat of Arms
The heraldic shield of a school, reflecting the vanity of the founder(s), with a design that is often intricate, and often incorporating animal symbolism. The shield is sometimes but not invariably aesthetically pleasing.

Coatees
Round, not particularly prepossessing boys' coats. These were fashionable in the 1860s, but forbidden at Eton, where the Eton suit continued to be worn.

College cap
See mortar board.

Colours
An award ostensibly for outstanding achievement in a school match against an outside team. This may take the form of a straw hat band, a sew-on badge, a special tie, etc. Sometimes colours are awarded purely to boost team spirit. A 'colour' also designates a schoolboy who has gained his colours.

Combinations
A single undergarment for body and legs, introduced in 1877. This lingered in some girls' schools through the first half of the twentieth century.

Cowshooters (Winchester)
Bowler hats.
Crinoline cage
A hooped petticoat worn by Victorian girls. Its discomfort subjugated their minds as well as their bodies. In an age of male chauvinism, this seemed only proper.
Dandy
A boy who has the means and inclination to dress foppishly. He usually hangs out in a fast set at his public school.
Drawers
An undergarment for body and legs, deriving from the ninth century. Drawers were first worn by little girls in the 1830s.
Ducker
Harrow's swimming pool.
Ducks (Harrow)
Football knickerbockers made of white duck.
Epaulettes
Ornamental shoulderpieces of cadet corps uniform.
Eton Block
Eton's portable wooden step over which boys bent to be flogged.
Eton jackets (also suit)
A short black jacket for younger boys, stopping just short of the buttocks. This was introduced in the late eighteenth century in various colours, and was worn at Eton and in the United States. It is still worn, for instance, at St. Paul's Cathedral Choir School on special occasions.
Fag
A public school junior who had to do menial, often trivial, tasks for a senior. If he was lucky, he was treated well in return. He often, however, suffered. Fagging has now been abolished.
Farthingale
A hooped petticoat, covered often with expensive materials.
Fez (Harrow)
A flat football cap with a long tassel attached to it.
Flannels (Harrow)
The grey flannel trousers worn by all Harrovians not entitled to the white cricket flannels.
Founders' Day
A day of commemoration, for which pupils wear their best schoolwear, e.g. Harrovians wear toppers, tailcoats and pinstripe trousers.
Gaberdine raincoat
A practical blue raincoat for schoolchildren, detested for its sexless drabness, and so recently superseded.
Gaiter
A covering of stiff khaki cloth, strapped around legs below the knee. This often slips, One gaiter is sometimes lost just before a parade, and turns out to have been 'borrowed' by another.
Good Godsters (Winchester)
Brown bowlers.

Gown (Academic)

A loose flowing black robe worn by masters on ceremonial occasions such as prize-giving or chapel, and in some schools actually for teaching. It does have the merit of keeping chalk from clothes. Some older masters delight in wearing tatty gowns. Gowns were originally awarded by universities. The Oxbridge versions are distinguishable from the redbrick. The academic gown probably derived from the earliest monastic habit, i.e. Benedictine.

Gym jocks

Baggy pants resembling pantaloons, worn for gym at Harrogate Ladies' College.

Habit

The dark, sometimes pleated robe of a monk or nun.

Harrow Football

A game peculiar to Harrow that contains elements of both rugger and soccer.

Hood

A separate head-covering garment worn over the academic gown.

House system

The division of a school into houses, each of which contains children of all ages. Usually, each house competes with the rest at sports, etc.

Housie

Informal wear at Christ's Hospital, and a welcome change from the charity dress.

Kirtle

A skirt worn by schoolgirls, approximately up to the end of the sixteenth century.

Kippers

Large round shoes secured by a strap, as worn at St. Joseph's Convent, Abbey Wood (1950s).

Liberty Bodice

A close-fitting under-bodice worn by girls under the age of twelve, up to the 1940s.

Montem Procession

A formal begging ceremony peculiar to Eton College that was abolished in 1844, in which pupils, dressed in military garb, would beg in the streets to raise money for the purpose of financing their school captain through Cambridge University.

Mortar Board (college cap)

The college cap derived from a soft square cap that sixteenth century Roman Catholic clergymen were accustomed to wearing. In time, it became so big that the edge had to be made rigid and raised from the crown, like a builder's mortar board – hence the name.

Motto

The epigram on a school arms, often in dubious Latin or Greek, offering some trite exhortation, usually religious, patriotic or both. Many school mottos are virtually interchangeable in terms of meaning.

Mufti

Plain clothes donned by boys who otherwise must wear uniform.

Navvies
Ironshod football boots, as once used at Rugby School.

Navvy Style
Wearing the school scarf in a bow over the neck. Pupils of King's School, Rochester have favoured this style while watching school matches, and it has now been forbidden there.

Norfolk Jacket
A loose jacket with box pleats and a conspicuous belt, worn by a few schoolboys into the early twentieth century, in imitation of their fathers' dress.

Panama Hat
Hat of fine pliant straw material, popularly worn by schoolgirls in summer. Pupils of Rochester Grammar School for Girls have traditionally tossed their panamas into the river on their last day there.

Pinafore
A girl's washable covering worn over a dress to protect from dust. This has sometimes been part of a uniform.

Pogging
A kind of fishing which entails wading in the water. This was practised at nineteenth century Stoneyhurst.

Pop (Eton)
A self-electing elite of older boys at Eton who have various privileges such as that of wearing fancy waistcoats. Members of Pop have often but not invariably shone at sports.

Popper
A member of Eton's Pop.

Porkpie Hat
A round felt hat, rarely worn in any school for long due to its unattractiveness.

Prizegiving
The annual ceremony for presentation of school prizes during which pupils are dressed in formal uniform, and teaching staff in gowns.

Puttees
A long strip of cloth wound spirally round the leg for extra protection. This is an obsolete precursor of the modern gaiter in cadet corps uniform. The word derives from the Hindu 'Patti', meaning band or bandage.

Scarf (Harrow)
House cricket and football colours.

Scholar
A pupil who through achievement in a competitive exam has earned himself/herself an education free, or at a reduced rate. The King's or Queen's Scholars have been appointed in accordance with principles of the original foundation.

Scruff Rig
Pupils' informal clothes worn after hours at the Royal Russell School, Purley.

Shag
Informal clothes at Westminster School, into which boarders may change after school.

Square
A square scarf worn by boys at King's School, Rochester, to indicate half colours.

Standard change (Eton College)
Jacket and tie. No jeans.

Stick-up Collars
See butterfly collars.

Stick-ups (Eton College)
A white bow tie and wing collar, worn by Etonians who have been successful in one or more of various activities.

Stocking
A tight covering, usually knitted or woven, for the foot and for part of the leg. Boys have worn these in special uniforms, e.g. the yellow stockings at Christ's Hospital. Girls have worn stockings more generally.

Straw (Harrow School)
The straw hat worn by the whole school all the year round, except at games and on Sundays.

Straw Yard
The epithet with which local yobs would taunt Compton Mackenzie as a schoolboy wearing a straw hat at St. Paul's Boys' School.

Surplice
A loose, full-sleeved white linen vestment, descending to knees or ankles. Choristers or King's Scholars wear this over the cassock at church services.

Tailcoat
A morning or evening coat with a long skirt, divided at the back into tails, and cut away in the front.

Tails (Harrow)
The swallow-tail coats once worn by all those in the Upper School, and by those over 5ft 6in. in the Lower School, where the coats were known as 'Charity Tails'.

Tap (Eton)
The College's own bar. This was made into a club to avoid licensing restrictions.

Topper
The top hat, still worn at Harrow School and at some choir schools. This has always been easily battered, and has been used to keep things in.

Trainers
Light shoes consisting of leather or suede uppers, and rubber soles. Children wear these for running and, increasingly, as fashionable leisure-wear. Popular makes include: Adidas, Puma, Nike, Hitec, Dunlop, and Diadora.

Trousers
These were introduced for boys in the 1770s, appearing either as tight long pantaloons, or in a shorter, wider style. At first considered childish, trousers soon ousted breeches.

Velour hat
Black felt headgear that can be pushed into a disrespectful shape.

Waistcoat
A boy's garment worn over the shirt, usually buttoned in front and sleeveless. It is worn under the jacket and is usually visible, e.g. the black waistcoat worn under the Eton tailcoat.

Wall Game
Eton College's own version of football, played against the traditional wall, in the course of which players' clothes usually end up torn and dirty.

Wet Bob (Eton)
Rower.

Wekker (Harrow)
Waistcoat.

Whiter (Harrow)
A white waistcoat, as was worn by those who had been three years in the school.

Yellow
Yellow waistcoat, as worn under the original Christ's Hospital cassock. The colour yellow was chosen instead of white in order to discourage vermin.

Bibliography

Chapter 1
The Dress of the English Schoolchild. Alan Mansfield. Costume Society Journal 1975.
The Historic Dress of the English Schoolboy. Society for the Preservation of Ancient Customs 1939.
English Girls' Boarding Schools. Mallory Wober. Allen Lane. The Penguin Press 1971.
Where 1967. 'Do you want school uniform?'
A Child of the Five Wounds. Antonia White. Essays by Diverse Hands. Ed. Graham Greene. Jonathan Cape 1934.
Whispering in the Rhododendrons. Arthur Marshall. Collins 1982.
Giggling in the Shrubbery. Arthur Marshall. Collins 1985.
Article 'Buying and Selling' by Miss Sheila Gould of Courtaulds. *Times Educational Supplement,* June 18, 1965.
The Public School Phenomenon. Jonathan Gathorne-Hardy. Hodder & Stoughton 1977.
Daily Telegraph Illustrated Supplement on Public Schools, November 14, 1932.
Chapter 2
Christ's Hospital. G.A. Allan 1984.
Charity Costumes. Phyllis Cunnington & Catherine Lucas. A & C Black Ltd. 1970.
A Short History of St. Martin in the Fields High School for Girls. D.H. Thomas 1929.
The Fable of the Bees (edn 1723). Bernard de Mandeville. York Grey Coat Girls' School. Bi-centenary souvenir. 1705-1905.
A Gentlemen's Magazine, June 1813.
The History of Sir Thomas Rich's School, Gloucester. D.J. Watkins, M.A.
Chapter 3
A History of Wellington College. David Newsome. John Murray 1959.
The Daily Telegraph, 1986.
Boys Together. Chapter 7. Fags and their Masters. John Chandos. O.U.P. 1985.
Boardroom Magazine. March-April 1986.
Chapter 4
People and Places. Richard Cobb. O.U.P. 1985.
Reminiscence by Sonia Wheal 75 Years of St. Paul's Girls' School. *The Daily Graphic.* Saturday, April 16th, 1904.

Memories of Edward Tyler (day boy, Kent College 1976-76). The Kent College Centenary Book. Christopher Wright. Batsford 1985.
A History of Chatham Grammar School for Girls 1907-1982. Audrey Perkyns. Meresborough Books 1982.
Downside By and Large. Dom Hubert Van Zeller. Steed & Ward 1954.
The Story of Highgate School. C.A. Evans. Chapman & Hall Ltd. 1949.
My Life & Times 1871-1900. Compton Mackenzie. Chatto & Windus 1963.
The Observer, December 1985.
Style in Clothes. James Laver. O.U.P. 1949.
The Psychology of Clothes. Flugel. The Hogarth Press 1930.
The First Term. The Portico Public School Magazine, No. IV - 1 February 1958.
Blue Coats into Blue Stockings. Louis Augers. Ian Allen Ltd. 1981.
'The Passing of Old School Cap.' Whitgift School Magazine. 1977.
Recollections of a Town boy at Westminster. Captain Markham. Edward Arnold 1903.
Downside By and Large. Van Zeller. Sheed & Ward 1954.

Chapter 5
The Language of Clothes. Alison Lurie. Heinemann 1983.
The Black Leather Jacket. Mike Farren. Plexus 1985.
A Sikh Family in Britain. W. Owen. Cole 1973.
Children's Clothes 1939-1970. Alice Guppy. Blandford Press Ltd. 1970.
Eton. A Dame's Chronicle. Nora Byron. William Kimber & Co. 1965.
How We Lived Then. Norman Longmate. Arrow Books 1971.
Giggling in the Shrubbery. Chapter 4. Clothes. Arthur Marshall. Collins 1985.

Chapter 6
Whispering in the Rhododendrons. Arthur Marshall. Collins 1982.
Children's Costume in England 1300-1900. Phyllis Cunnington & Anne Buck. A & C Black 1965.
The History of Underclothes. C. Willet & Phyllis Cunnington. Michael Joseph Ltd. 1951.
Elizabeth Ham. By Herself. 1783-1820. (1945).
Minute Books. Harper Trust. 1764-1833. Beds County Office.
Glenvervie Journals (1811). Ed. F. Bickley 1928.
A Dictionary of English Costume. 900-1900. C. Willett Cunnington, Phyllis Cunnington & Charles Beard. Adam & Charles Black 1960.
Blue (Colour) Skirts & Blue Stockings. Louis Angus. W.H. Allen Ltd. 1981.
10 Years in a Comprehensive School. Stephen King.
Article 'Don't say bra, say bust bodice'. *Guardian* Woman, May 17th 1982.
History of Oxford Central Girls' School & Cheney Girls' Grammar School. M. Spackman. Published privately 1974.

Chapter 7
*Downside By & Large.*Dom Hubert Van Zeller. Sheen & Ward 1954.
Eton. A Dame's Chronicle. Nora Byron. William Kimber & Co. Ltd. 1965.
A History of the First Hundred Years of the Rugby School Corps 1860-1960. Lieutenant-Colonel H.J. Harris, T.D., D.L.
Cadets at Giggleswick 1912-1980. Published by Giggleswick School.

Recollections of Schooldays at Harrow. Rev. H.J. Torre. Manchester 1890.

Blue Skirts & Blue Stockings. Louis Anger. Ian Allen Ltd. 1981.

The History of Ayton School. The Jubilee Committee 1891.

Boys Together. John Chandos. O.U.P. 1985.

A Short History of English Schools, 1750-1965. Christopher Martin, Watland Publishers Ltd. 1979.

The Kindling and the Flame. A Centenary Review of the History of South Hampstead High School. By Prunella R. Bodington.

Kent College. A Centenary. Christopher Wright. Batsford.

Royal Russell School. A History. S. Hopewell. Hutchinson Benham Ltd. 1978.

Stratford Revisited. Bradford Girls' Grammar School. The Centenary Edition of the School Magazine. 1875-1975.

Chapter 8

Eton. How It Works. J.D.R. McConnell. Faber & Faber.

History of Children's Costume. Elizabeth Ewing. Batsford 1977.

A Short History of Public Schools. Christopher Martin. Wayland Publishers Ltd. 1979.

Class. Chapter 4. Education. Jilly Cooper. Methuen 1979.

A Country Ramble. The Williamsonian. No. I. Feb. 1885.

Boring Never. The Memoirs of Margaret E. Popham-Johnson. London 1968.

Chapter 9

Eton. How it Works. J.D.R. McConnell. Faber & Faber 1967.

Giggling in the Shrubbery. Arthur Marshall. Collins 1985.

Downside By and Large. Van Zeller. Sheed & Ward 1954.

The Kent College Centenary Book. Christopher Wright. Batsford 1985.

An Eton Schoolboy's Album. Debrett's Peerage Ltd. 1985.

Memoir by Alison Adburgham (née Haig). No. 4. 1925-29.

The History of Emanuel School 1594-1964. C.W. Scott-Giles & B.V. Slater. The Old Emanuel Association.

Recollections of Schooldays at Harrow. The Rev. H.J. Torre. Manchester 1890.

Uncommon Entrance. Edward Blishen. Thames & Hudson 1974.

The Greeks. H.D.F. Kitto. Penguin 1951.

A School's Adventure. C.W. Olive. Sheen & Ward 1944.

Bishops Stortford College 1868-1968. A Centenary Chronicle. J.M. Dent & Sons Ltd. 1969.

The History of Radley College. 1847-1947. A.K. Boyd. Basil Blackwell, Oxford 1948.

'Boy Made Man.' Peregrine Worsthorne. *The World of the Public School.* Introduced by G.M. Fraser. Weidenfeld & Nicholson 1977.

'Potting Shed of the English Rose.' E. Arnot Robertson. *The Old School.* Ed. Graham Greene. O.U.P. 1984.

The Schools for the People 1871.

The Teacher, January 22, 1971.

Times Educational Supplement 1966.

Chapter 10
'75 Years of St. Paul's School'. *The Daily Graphic.* Saturday, April 16th 1904.
'Bradford Girls' Grammar School' – The Centenary edition of The School Magazine 1875-1975.
Memoires of the late J.C. Hosking (K.C. 1899-1905). The Kent College Centenary Book. Christopher Wright. Batsford Ltd. 1985.
Reminiscences of George Gilbert. Privately printed. Archives, The King's School, Canterbury.
Giggling in the Shrubbery. Arthur Marshall. Collins 1985.
Chapter 11
'Manners Makyth Man.' Tim Brooke-Taylor. *The World of the Public School.* Weidenfeld & Nicholson 1977.
Reminiscences of a Public Schoolboy. W.N. Marcy. 1932.
In All Their Glory. John Nettleton. AMA 1970.
'Child of the Five Wounds', *The Old School.* Ed. Graham Greene. Jonathan Cape 1934.
Whispering in the Shrubbery. Arthur Marshall. Collins 1985.
'Rutherford. An Appreciation.' R.N. Campbell. *The Elizabethan.* December 1941.
Boys Together. English Public Schools 1880-1964. John Chandos. O.U.P. 1984.
'The Teacher'. January 22, 1971.
The Millstone Race. David Briggs 1983.
The History of the Elephant Man. Michael Howell & Peter Ford. Allison & Busby 1980.
The History of Radley College 1847-1947. A.K. Boyd. Basil Blackwell. Oxford 1948.
Article by Nevil Johnson. *Where* 1964.
Chapter 12
A Better Class of Person. John Osborne. Penguin.
The Girl's Guide to the English Public Schoolboy. Rebecca Irvine. Severn House.
The Loom of Youth. Alec Waugh.
Fielding Gray. Simon Raven. Anthony Blond Ltd.
'Charlie Collingwood's Flogging by Etoniensis' by Swinburne. Originally published in *The Pearl.*
The Cement Garden. Ian McKewen. Picador.
Carrie. Stephen King. New English Library.
Kes. Barry Hines. Penguin.
Cider with Rosie. Laurie Lee. Penguin.
Portrait of the Artist as a Young Man. James Joyce.
Chapter 14
A History of Football. M. Marple. 1954.
English Costume for Sports & Recreation. Phyllis Cunnington & Alan Mansfield. A & C Black Ltd. 1969.
Beaumont. 1861-1961. Peter Levi.
The History of Radley College 1847-1947. A.K. Boyd. Basil Blackwell 1948.
St. Omer to Stonyhurst. Hubert Chadwick. S.J. Burns & Bates 1962.

History of Stonyhurst College. Craggers & Keating. Kegan Paul, Trench, Tribner & Co. Ltd. 1981.
Eton. A Dame's Chronicle. Nora Byron. William Kimber & Co. 1965.
*English Costume for Sports & Recreation.*Ch. 6. Tennis. Phyllis Cunnington & Alan Mansfield.
'Bedales Pioneers'. E.L. Grant. *The Old School.* Ed. Graham Greene. Jonathan Cape 1934.
A World Apart. Daphne Rae. The Lutterworth Press 1983.
The Royal Naval School. Philip Unwin 1976.
Jennings' Little Hut. Anthony Buckeridge. Collins.
My Kingdom for a Horse. W. Allison 1919.
English Costume for Sports and Recreation. Chapter 3, Football. Phyllis Cunnington & Alan Mansfield. A & C Black Ltd. 1969.
'The Conformer (Harrow).' L.P. Hartley. *The Old School.* Ed. Graham Greene. Jonathan Cape 1934.
Mr. Olim. Ernest Raymond. Cassell 1961.
Shrewsbury School, Recent Years. J.M. Pendlebury & J.M. West. Wilding & Son 1934.
The Language of Clothes. Alison Lurie. Heinemann 1981.
Eton. How it Works. J.D.R. McConnell. Faber & Faber 1967.
Eton. A Dame's Chronicle. Nora Byron. William Kimber & Co. Ltd. 1965.
Times Educational Supplement. 4 February 1955.
The Dualogues of Juan Luis Vives. Translated by Foster Watson. Frank Can & Co. Ltd.
Chapter 15
Boy. Roald Dahl.
Such Such Were the Joys. George Orwell.
Goodbye to All That. Robert Graves.
The English Gentleman. Simon Raven. Anthony Blond Ltd. 1961.
'Grammar School'. H.E. Bates. *The Old School.* Jonathan Cape 1934.
Conundrum. Jan Morris. Faber & Faber 1974.
A Sort of Life. Graham Greene. The Bodley Head 1971.
Blushes. Supplement No. 7. Broadway Publishing 1986.
The Historic Dress of the English Schoolboy. Rev. Wallace Clare. The Society for the Preservation of Ancient Costumes 1939.
Old School Tie (Introduction). Penguin 1965.
Chapter 16
Christ's Hospital. G.A.T. Allan. London 1984.
Graham Street Memories. Edited by Beatrix Durning.
History of Sidcot School 1808-1908.
Unbroken Community. The Glory of the Friends' School, Saffron Walden. 1701-1932. David W. Bolam. W. Heffer & Sons Ltd. 1952.
Summerhill. A.S. Neill. Victor Golancz 1962.
Locked Up Daughters. F. Lamb & H. Picthorn. Hodder & Stoughton 1960.
Article: 'Nuns Retreat from Habits of the Past'. Carmel Fitzsimons. *The Observer,* Sunday 2 February 1986.
Through the Narrow Gate. A Nun's Story. Karen Armstrong. Macmillan London Ltd. 1981.

Old Public Schools of England. John Rogers. Batsford 1938.
Chapter 17
The sex life letters from the pages of *Forum*. Forum Press 1972.
'My Brother' and *'On Suicide'*. Thomas de Quincey.
'Beating in Britain'. *The New Statesman*, 29 November 1968.
The English Woman's Domestic Magazine 1867-1870.
Down with Skool. Geoffrey Williams & Ronald Searle. Max Parish & Co. Ltd. 1958.
Boys Together. English Public Schools 1800-1864. John Chandos.
The English Vice – beating, sex and shame in Victorian England and After. Duckworth & Co. Ltd. 1978.
Floreat Etona, Anecdotes & Memories of Eton College. Ralph Nevill 1911.
The Public School Phenomenon. Jonathan Gathorne-Hardy. Hodder & Stoughton 1977.
The Naked Ape. 1967. Desmond Morris.
Beyond Freedom and Dignity. B.F. Skinner. Jonathan Cape 1982.
'Manners Makyth Man'. Tim Brooke-Taylor. *The World of the Public School.* Weidenfeld and Nicholson 1977.
'Indian Innocence'. Derek Verschoyle. *The Old School.* Ed. Graham Greene. Jonathan Cape 1934.
Introduction by George MacDonald Fraser. *The World of the Public School.* Weidenfeld & Nicholson 1977.
'Reminiscence of Jean Dransfield 1924-1936'. Bradford Girls' Grammar School. The Centenary Edition of the School Magazine, 1875-1975.
The Psychology of Clothes. J.C. Flugel. The Hogarth Press 1930.

INDEX